NATIONAL GEOGRAPHIC

PHOTOGRAPHING
BIRDS

NATIONAL GEOGRAPHIC

PHOTOGRAPHING
BIRDS

RULON E. SIMMONS WITH BATES LITTLEHALES

A Bald Eagle swoops toward the
photographer, who fires a camera
with a 300mm lens plus a 2x extender.
The larger the bird, the better the
chances for flight shots—unless the
large bird flies as fast as this one.

NATIONAL GEOGRAPHIC
WASHINGTON, D.C.

CONTENTS

Opposite page: A Little Blue Heron stalks food in a pond covered with water lettuce. The dense pattern of plants provides an interesting background and vivid contrast to the bird.

PREFACE

I'm an unabashed birder, and although I've concentrated on painting birds, my camera is always with me in the field. I use my photographs for reference, almost like a second notebook with entries on bird poses, lighting conditions, and feather details (when I can get close enough!). The interests of birders and nature photographers are far-ranging. You might be focused on a completely different path—landscapes with birds, behavioral studies, birds in flight, documenting rare birds—or you might prefer to concentrate on a specific group of birds or a special place. Possibilities abound.

One thing we share is a desire to take excellent photographs of birds. Birds are challenging subjects, and some of the skills needed to capture them on film or pixels are specialized ones. You might eventually figure out what you need to know through trial and error. I muddled along for years, getting a few good shots and wasting a lot of film——not really knowing what I was doing wrong or how to improve. The process would have been much smoother and the learning curve much steeper with a book like this one to guide me.

Whether you are an experienced photographer seeking suggestions on how to improve your bird images or a birder just getting started in photography, the sage advice of two veteran bird photographers—Rulon E. Simmons and Bates Littlehales—resides within these covers, ready to help you. You'll find excellent guidance on equipment (including the latest in digital technology), lighting and exposure, how to get close to your subjects, and even some of the authors' favorite shooting locations. The birds are out there!

—*Jonathan Alderfer*

A male Rose-breasted Grosbeak alit on a prefocused branch over a drip pool. There was only time to shoot one frame, then he was gone.

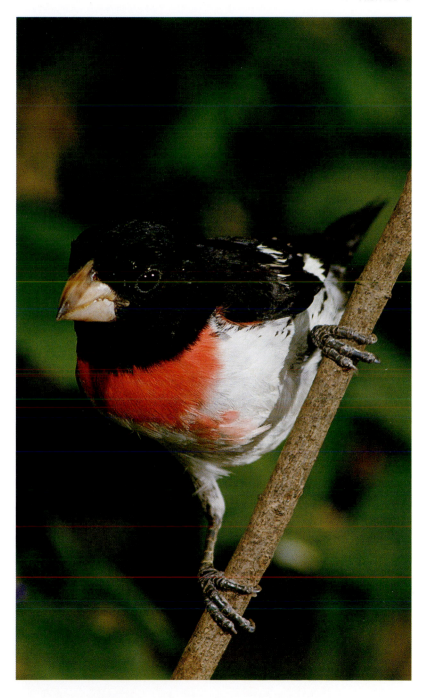

RULON E. SIMMONS

Have you ever wondered how the experts take fantastic pictures of wildlife? Their photography may particularly amaze you if you have ever tried to approach a bird or other small animal, only to have it fly or run away before you could even get close to it. In this book, you'll find the secrets of bird photography that I have discovered through research, experimentation, and lots of practical experience in the field.

This guide is designed to be helpful to amateur and serious nature photographers as well as bird-watchers (most prefer to be called birders) who want to pursue their interests through photography. It features photographic techniques, tips for getting close to birds, suggestions of great locations for finding "photographable" birds, and species-specific suggestions for getting outstanding pictures of birds. It also features many photographs, along with helpful information about how they were taken.

For more than 30 years, I have been interested in photography, particularly nature photography. During much of that time, I took photographs of flowers, large mammals, insects, and amphibians, with only an occasional photograph of a bird. Like many other photographers, I had the misconception that it was necessary to put up a blind at a nest to get good pictures of birds.

Putting up a blind requires considerable time and knowledge of bird behavior. It also risks upsetting birds while they are nesting. Nevertheless, in many publications on bird photography, the emphasis has been on this very technique.

I have since discovered that bird pictures can be taken using a variety of techniques, many of which are much easier than setting up a blind at a nest. Faster and sharper films, better camera equipment, and now digital photography have opened up a wide range of possibilities. I'll outline a number of different ways to get good bird pictures with various types of equipment.

The keys to successful bird photography include the proper selection of equipment, knowledge of good locations for photography, some understanding of animal behavior, and good timing. Each of these will be discussed in the pages of this book.

Using a combination of techniques described here, you should be able to take good bird pictures just about anywhere during all seasons of the year. With practice, I have been able to photograph well over 300 species of birds in my spare time.

Visiting locations, such as certain wildlife refuges, will enhance your opportunities for successful bird photography. I've included some of my favorite sites in the United States and Canada.

In writing this bird photography field guide, I hope to show readers that bird photography need not remain the hobby of just a dedicated and persevering few, but can be enjoyed by all with a reasonable amount of effort.

Bird photography can be equally satisfying whether you approach it as an avid photographer or an avid birder. It brings me double joy because my strong interest in photography joins a fascination with birds, engendered by a father who was an ornithologist.

BATES LITTLEHALES

Most people have heard the expression "free as a bird." Poetic as it may sound, it inaccurately describes the real life of a bird, who is governed by all sorts of rules and regulations put upon it by nature.

Some knowledge of these restrictions enables a bird photographer to think more like a bird than like a hunter trying to make a trophy shot of an elusive subject. Amassing this knowledge can be a lifetime quest. But it quickly shows up in your photography as marked improvement.

When I started out, I was thrilled just to get a sharp, colorful image of a bird. But I realized that editors wanted more than that. They wanted action and personality, behavior and excitement. They couldn't tell me how to get all this, but that's what they wanted. Fortunately, I had access to experts in the field of ornithology and a background in the frantic pursuit of people photography plus sports—valuable experience for shooting pictures of birds, who are only occasionally frozen into still lifes.

My fascination with birds dates back to age 13 and never waned until romance and military experience demanded so much of my time. Now I'm back to birds, without sacrificing the romance. Above all, though, I made time for trial and error. And patience? Let's call it maturation and interest.

Study, rather than try to compete with, the work of other bird photographers. Also study what wildlife painters do with birds: how they integrate them into compositions, into habitats and landscapes, how they hint at action and personality within the limitations of a still format.

Always remember that you are exploiting birds to photograph them. Exploitation need not be all bad. If you supply food and water, it's win-win exploitation. If you interrupt rhythms of courtship and nesting by your intrusion, it's bad exploitation. Awareness of the bird's life history will guide your ethics. When you think your photo is more important than consideration of the bird, you've become one of the bird "paparazzi." Editors might pay well for intruding on movie stars. But birds? Doubtful.

Perhaps you'll use your photography to collect new species, just as you would tick them off on your life list. I met a man in the field once who wouldn't list any bird he hadn't photographed. Game playing—but what fun!

Whatever photo games you play, keep an open mind for new approaches. Don't just play it safe with tried-and-true formulas. Take chances. Remember the cardinal rule of photography: "Thou shalt not bore thine audience." Birds have attitudes and their actions and postures show these attitudes. Blue Jays, for instance, remind my wife of grand opera stars, overacting at every opportunity. Mourning Doves appear serene by comparison. Try to inject the same quality of life into your photographs that these marvelous little kinetic sculptures show you in the field.

If you do not immediately set the bird photography world afire, blame me. I'm responsible for the little boxes called "tips" that you will find throughout this book.

WHAT MAKES A GREAT BIRD PHOTOGRAPH?

Understanding and working with bird behavior leads to more interesting bird photographs, but who's to say that great bird images must be filled with extreme action? A mockingbird "scaring" its prey with uplifted wings makes a strong image, but so does a robin with head cocked, looking (not listening!) for a worm.

A master duck decoy carver really has to know his birds, or else he can't abstract their forms and gestures convincingly. To do exceptional work, the bird photographer has the same responsibility.

The image must be a powerful photograph to be an exceptional bird study. It must be composed well, but not necessarily in a conventional way. All the elements within the frame must work together without distractions to misguide the eye. Conventional rules are helpful, but don't become a slave to them. A photograph should be as sharp as possible, unless intentionally unsharp (blurring to suggest movement sometimes works, but just as often doesn't). Tonal contrast must be pleasing, to give a clean look to the picture. Use available light and time of day to your advantage.

An Altamira Oriole, above, has plumage that screams "Look at me!" Often color alone is enough to dramatize a bird photograph—an attitude of impending action is a bonus. Opposite, the setting sun silhouettes an American Coot. The light takes the image beyond the ordinary without sacrificing the main idea—a water bird integrated into its habitat.

What do you want the photograph to say? Some statements are pure bird messages: This goldfinch eats seeds from a thistle plant. Some are more anthropomorphic: This hawk is fierce—you can see it in his eye. Show your message as clearly as

A dark background sets off the Anhinga in this photograph (below), giving the image a dramatic quality. The twisted curves of both the bird and the log are key elements in this composition.

This Wild Turkey (opposite) paused just long enough to allow a head shot—one frame only. The photographer used a close-focusing 300mm lens as well as a 2x tele-extender.

possible. The goldfinch must be cracking the seed, not just looking at it.

Do everything you can to enhance the mood or feeling in your image. A lone gull in heavy fog creates a very different mood from a flock of gulls against a bright blue sky. I once made a photograph of a bird whose habitat was shallow water. In a drought, he was legging it across a dry, cracked plain. The mood? Heartbreaking.

Study bird lore and photo technique. Keep your statement bold and full of life—and stay open to occasional accidents that could help make your bird images great.

—BATES LITTLEHALES

A little action adds great interest to this shot of a Trumpeter Swan drying off after a bath (above). After a dip, waterfowl predictably rise up and flap their wings, providing opportunities for action shots. Knowledge of bird behavior increases your chances of capturing great moments on film. A tight crop of a preening Northern Gannet pair (below) enhances the intimacy of the moment.

A Tricolored Heron stands out against a subtle background (above). The curves of the bird's perch mirror the curves of its neck.

Following pages: Bird photographs need not be close-ups to be successful. This image sets a peaceful mood by using the sweep of landscape and time of day to show a duck completely at home in its habitat.

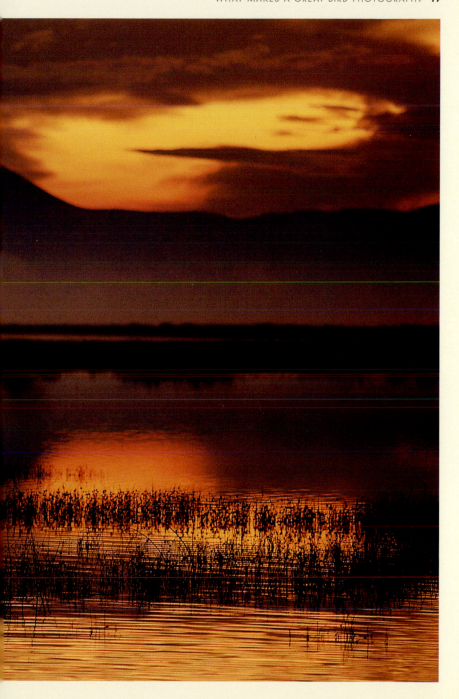

CHAPTER ONE
GETTING STARTED

CAMERA EQUIPMENT

Clearly, before you can begin in bird photography, you must have some equipment. What should you buy? How much equipment is really necessary? What film should you use? Let's take a look.

Today's 35mm single-lens reflex (SLR) cameras have become the cameras of choice for most bird photographers. For these cameras, a wide variety of accessories is available to accommodate the bird photographer's needs. Large- and medium-format cameras and their lenses are much more expensive and very heavy to lug into the field.

Cameras smaller than 35mm are generally not suitable for bird photography because they lack the long lenses necessary to get good pictures. Furthermore, the image quality is marginal at best with these small cameras. The obvious choice for most photographers will be a 35mm SLR camera. A number of good brands and models are currently available.

To be suitable for bird photography, the camera must be able to accommodate interchangeable lenses, allowing for the use of a long focal-length lens. Beyond that main requirement, several other optional camera features should be given consideration. A built-in light meter or expertise with a hand-held meter that measures incident light can make a big difference. With either of these, precise exposures can be obtained quickly under variable lighting conditions. A motor drive or autowinder is a nice accessory for nature photography. Having one will allow you to concentrate

Multiple flashes made possible this image of a Winter Wren foraging on a shaded bank. The area—not the wren itself—had to be lit with flash, since the small bird was in constant motion.

more on the subject and let you take additional exposures in rapid succession if necessary.

If you're using a consumer-grade digital camera, make sure it has a long enough zoom lens range to allow portraits of birds. Also, digital cameras that offer built-in image stabilization will help ensure sharper pictures.

LENSES

Two lenses will satisfy most situations bird photographers will encounter. Without doubt, the most useful lens for bird photography is a telephoto with a focal length of 400mm or greater. I use such a lens for at least 90 percent of my bird photography. A zoom lens in the range of 70 to 300mm works well for photographing birds that can be approached closely, as from behind a blind. Much of the bird photography that can be done without the use of a blind requires longer focal length lenses, usually in the 500 to 600mm range.

It's surprising how close you have to get to a bird to fill the frame, even with such long lenses. You can use lenses longer than 600mm, but with increasing difficulty. First, a longer lens tends to exaggerate camera vibration and subject motion. With a longer lens, there's also more physical distance between you and your subject. The atmosphere in between will often have a degrading effect on your pictures. Longer lenses are generally slower and require the use of faster films or a heavy, steady tripod.

Long telephoto lenses come in two main types: refractive lenses, composed of several refracting glass lens elements, and catadioptric lenses, consisting of a couple of mirror elements as well as refracting lens elements. Catadioptric lenses have the advantage of being much more compact. They can also be less expensive. Some people, however, dislike the doughnut-shaped highlights characteristic of these lenses. Another drawback is that most

TIP

Explore the possibilities by varying your approach to any given species of bird. What will a high viewpoint convey? A head-on shot? Just pretend you're shooting a photo essay, and don't get stuck on the same approach.

Three pictures of Harlequin Ducks, all equally valid, convey three different messages. Progressing from a normal focal-length lens (top) to a medium telephoto, to a 500mm lens (bottom), the photographer shows: a bird in landscape, a bird in its habitat, and a courting pair.

catadioptric lenses have a fixed aperture, which provides potentially less precise exposure control and no control over depth of field. Longer lenses suitable for bird photography must sacrifice depth of field for adequate shutter speed.

A good telephoto lens need not cost a fortune. I have had very good results with two moderately priced lenses. I started out in bird photography using a 450mm lens. Later, I added a 70-210mm zoom lens to my inventory. As budget and circumstances have allowed, I have shifted to longer 600 and 1,000mm lenses, which enable me to take pictures of birds at greater distances. Secondhand lenses are an option, too. Newer lenses with more "bells and whistles" leave some fine older lenses on the used market.

Lenses purchased from third-party vendors can cost considerably less than those purchased from camera manufacturers. The optical quality of most

TIP

Buy the best lenses you can afford, but be aware of their limitations. Making large prints is very demanding on optics, a living-room slide show less so. If you use tele-extenders, buy ones designed for particular lenses, not "all-purpose" ones.

In-camera meters have no intelligence whatsoever. They can only accurately register medium tones. The photographer metered the Great Egret and compensated for the exposure in this photo (opposite). If you meter the dark background, it will wash out to medium gray. The bird will be overexposed and lose detail (top). If you meter the snow-white bird, it will turn gray (bottom).

of today's telephoto lenses is very good, though barrel construction and mechanical parts may vary in quality from one manufacturer to another.

Another significant factor in lens cost is the maximum aperture of the lens. Lenses with a larger aperture will let in more light, allowing photography under more difficult conditions of illumination and motion. But the larger the aperture, the higher the cost. If you purchase a long lens with an f-number in the range of f/5.6 to f/8, you should be able to do an adequate job with most of your bird photography. A wider aperture lens (an f/4, for instance) will cost considerably more. Whenever possible, it is a good idea to field-test a lens before buying it to make sure it will meet your expectations.

EXTENSION TUBES AND BELLOWS
Older telephoto lenses often will not focus close enough for close-ups of small birds such as sparrows.

You can remedy this by using extension tubes or bellows, which move the near-focus distance closer to the camera. Bellows allow for a greater range of adjustment more quickly than is possible with extension tubes. The drawback is that bellows are more delicate and clumsier to manipulate.

When using extension tubes or bellows, remember to make an appropriate exposure adjustment, if necessary. This adjustment occurs automatically when the exposure is metered through the lens, either for ambient light or through-the-lens (TTL) flash metering. TTL flash usually applies to on-camera flash equipment that uses a hot shoe.

For situations where metering through the camera is not possible, you'll have to increase the exposure to compensate for the effective increase in f-number created by the tubes or bellows. Instructions with the extension equipment should

In 1961, when these Inca Terns were photographed in Peru, catadioptric lenses were more commonly used. The relatively lightweight 500mm lens had a maximum aperture of only f/8, and did wild things to reflected light on the sea in the background.

tell you how much to change the exposure for different amounts of extension.

The use of extension tubes requires you to compensate with the exposure. Experiment beforehand to determine your light loss with a favorite lens-tube combination. Fortunately, modern telephoto lenses generally focus much closer than their older counterparts and will not require extensions for most applications.

There are times in the field when, even with a long-focal-length lens, you'll be too far away for good pictures. At such times, you can use a tele-converter to extend the focal length of the lens. A 1.4x converter works well and only loses one f-stop. A 2x converter will double the focal length and make the bird appear twice as close, but it costs two f-stops and could cause vignetting.

Sometimes a photographer will be able to get so close to a bird that, except for head shots or details, a longer lens is no longer suitable. Then the variable-focal-length zoom lens in the range of 70-300mm comes in handy. Unlike early zoom lenses, the quality of most of today's lenses is very good. Fortunately, the prices are also much more attractive than they used to be.

EXPOSURE

Built-in light meters in most 35mm cameras today make getting the proper exposure quite easy. Some cameras select the exposure automatically; others require adjustment by centering a needle or reading an LED display. You'll need to compensate, however, when the bird is significantly lighter or darker than its surroundings. For example, a bird against a light sky will usually come out under-exposed if you're using the camera's exposure meter reading. In such cases, you'll need to increase the exposure by one or two stops to compensate for the meter reading that is unduly influenced by the lighter sky.

TIP

When varying from tried-and-true techniques and moving into new technical territory, work through problems at home. Don't wait until you are in the field. Keep a notebook to help you remember what works and what doesn't.

An overcast sky can be brighter than a white reflector (a white reflector having a reflectance of about 70-80 percent). This causes problems for a meter designed for a scene of around 12.5 percent reflectance. The problem is worse for a very dark bird against an overcast sky, and will require more exposure adjustment. A clear blue sky is less of a problem. If a light-colored bird is against a darker background, generally one half stop less exposure than indicated by the light meter will produce good results.

One way to get a better light reading for difficult exposure situations is to take a reading off the ground rather than off the bird. A handheld incident meter can also be used to get a proper exposure reading.

FLASH PHOTOGRAPHY

When circumstances call for flash photography, the flash must at least provide enough light for adequate exposure when the lens is at its widest aperture. Preferably, the flash will provide even more illumination so that the lens can be stopped down to smaller apertures for increased depth of field. A special light-focusing lens called a Fresnel lens can be used with a flash to concentrate more light on the subject.

In flash photography, there will always be a main light. A second flash can serve as fill to lighten shadows. A third flash may be necessary to illuminate the background. All units except the one plugged into the camera will need slaves to fire them. A slave is a photoelectric device that plugs into the flash and causes it to fire when it "sees" light from another flash. Many cameras include built-in wireless triggering that works with flash units via infrared beams.

Diffused flash will be gentler than direct flash. Gauze or commercial diffusers help create softer,

Frozen in mid-flight by a high-speed flash, this Carolina Chickadee broke an infrared beam projected from a receiver programmed to trigger the camera. The ratio of good images to failures is low with this technique.

A Gray Catbird, attracted to the photographer's backyard drip pool, bathes with such rapid movements that a high-speed flash was needed to capture the details.

more natural lighting. If you use multiple flash heads, a flash meter will prove to be another important accessory. The flash meter will tell you exactly how much light your subject will receive from the combined flashes.

Other handy items you might want to consider include ballheads, quick releases, and cable releases. Ballheads attach directly under your lens mount and allow for quick changes in the lens position in any direction, but they may not be suitable for extremely large lenses. Quick releases permit fast removal of the lens from the tripod without having to unscrew the support. Cable releases, either manual or electronic, trip the shutter with a minimum of disturbance to the camera, thus reducing the possibility of vibration. The flop of the mirror in an SLR is the worst culprit, even with a release and tripod. The worst shutter speed for mirror flop in many cameras is one-eighth of

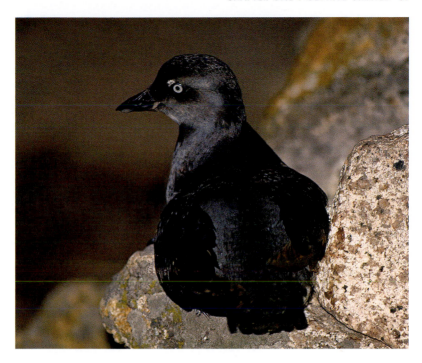

a second. Tests with your own camera and lens will help you determine what it is for yours.

Image-stabilizing lenses, which facilitate handholding at slower shutter speeds, are also available. This exciting new technology helps eliminate the need for a tripod in many situations. A general rule of thumb for hand-holding a lens is to use a speed at least as fast as the focal length. The new technology allows the photographer to use a slower shutter speed, which in turn allows the lens to be stopped down as much as two stops.

TRIPODS

A sturdy tripod is an important piece of equipment for bird photographers. Use a tripod with lenses longer than about 300mm. Get a model that has sufficient height extension to enable you to photograph birds in trees from a comfortable standing position. A quick-release that screws into the

Cassin's Auklet only comes ashore at night. The situation called for more punch than on-camera flash could normally deliver. A Fresnel lens in front of the flash focused the light and provided additional f-stops.

Following pages:
To bird-biased viewers, this is a photo of dowitchers feeding in a marsh. To others, it could be a landscape ornamented by birds. Whatever the point of view, the image must work as a strong photo to command attention.

lens mount allows for efficient attachment to the tripod as you set up for a shot. Better tripods offer a choice of heads, each with different mechanics.

FILM

After selecting a camera and lens, you'll need to choose your film. The first consideration is whether to use color slide or color negative film. Most photographers choose slide film for book or magazine reproduction and for presentations. Many also prefer the quality of slides for general nature photography (slide film will give greater tonal range between lights and darks than is possible in a print). Photographers usually choose negative film when they want prints only.

Every photographer has one or more favorite films. For many years, Kodachrome was my favorite for nature photography. Kodachrome films have very good resolving power and excellent speed-grain relationships.

More recently, I have done most of my bird photography with the newer Elite Chrome 200 film. This film gives relatively high speed with quality previously associated only with slower films. Furthermore, it pushes very well up to three stops for use in extremely challenging conditions. For flight photographs, I usually push this film to E.I. 320. Pushed Elite Chrome 200 provides great results, maintaining excellent color balance without building up too much contrast or film grain.

An ISO 50 speed film is at the lower threshold of suitability for most bird photography. Photographers with very fast, generally expensive lenses use films in this range. But even then, they often push these films another stop to get the necessary speed to avoid blurred pictures. By using a little faster film, one can get a higher percentage of good pictures, often while using less expensive lenses. This helps in low-light conditions or when shooting birds in flight.

TIP

Hand-holding long lenses gives more freedom to quickly relate foreground to background, but the technique requires lots of practice.

To blur or not to blur? The use of a slow-speed flash produces an impressionistic image of a Common Redpoll (above), capturing the feeling of flight. The White-breasted Nuthatch (below) was stopped by high-speed flash.

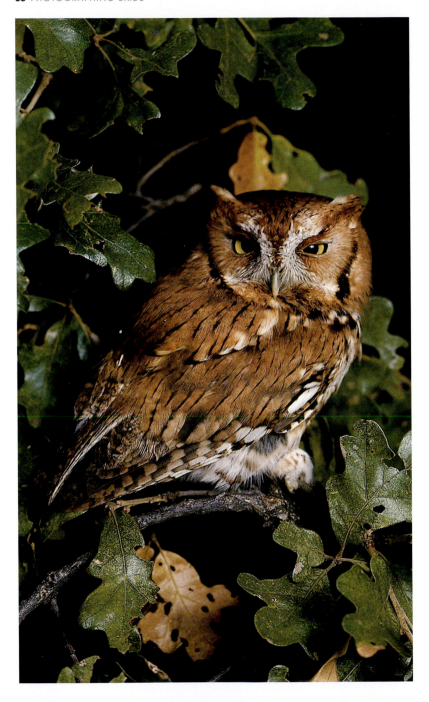

Since bird photographers usually work with long lenses that magnify motion of active birds and have relatively shallow depth of field, the extra speed can also be helpful even under full-sun conditions. Faster-speed films will allow you to increase the shutter speed, which helps stop motion, thereby reducing the chance that camera or subject motion will ruin the picture. Alternatively, you can decrease aperture size, which increases the depth of field.

There are many kinds of film on the market. In choosing one, consider qualities such as film speed, sharpness, film grain, and color rendition. Test different films under different conditions to become familiar with their characteristics. Select a film speed that works well with your equipment. Decide whether you prefer accurate colors or the more saturated colors provided by some of today's films. With testing and practice, you'll find a high-quality film that best meets your needs and suits your own style of photography.

BUYING DIGITAL

The digital SLR cameras (DSLRs), which feed images into a computer or other electronic storage device instead of generating transparencies or negatives through film, are now valuable tools for bird photography. Until the DSLRs that accommodate interchangeable lenses became available and affordable, the consumer-level digital cameras remained marginal for bird work. While great for all sorts of other photography, they just don't have the flexibility birds demand.

Most birds do not trust human beings. The bird photographer who ignores this general truism does so at his or her photographic peril. The stronger telephoto lens, even from a blind, levels the mistrust playing field somewhat. Without that extra focal length—from 300 to 600mm—the bird shooter is at a considerable disadvantage.

TIP
Printing through a computer to a photo-quality printer can give stunning results from either slides or color negatives.

This Eastern Screech-Owl was lit by a single flash, diffused by bouncing the light off a white reflective surface. Often multiple flashes are impractical, and measures must be taken to mitigate the harshness of a single light. As long as the reflective surface, used in this case as the light source, is larger than the subject, the light should be soft enough.

The tools for the 35mm discussed earlier in this chapter also pertain to the DSLR with several exceptions. One obvious exception is the lack of film. Say goodbye to those familiar little rolls that were the staples of your picture-making life. You'll find it liberating! Gone are the waiting for lab processing and the gloom of the darkroom. Gone is airport anxiety over x-rays. With today's digital cameras, for most applications, you won't be sacrificing any image quality by switching from film to digital.

Another notable difference is the LCD monitor. With this new tool you can immediately check the exposure, lighting, composition, and, to some extent, sharpness of the picture you just made. If you're unhappy with the results, you can simply delete the frame from the camera storage. Unlike some non-DSLR cameras that have rotating LCD panels that act as view finders as well as monitors, DSLRs have through-the-lens viewing; the LCD panels merely act as monitors, showing the image after the picture has been taken.

A bird photographer can appreciate the complexity inside a DSLR, such as this Canon, without having to understand it. It is crucial, however, to understand that, since the sensor is smaller than 35mm frames, the 35mm-designed lenses give up to 1.5 times the magnification—a plus for the bird photographer.

All digital cameras use image sensors to capture pictures. A sensor is a light-sensitive electronic microprocessor that sits behind the lens. When the camera is turned on, the sensor responds to light and affects the flow of electricity through it, depending on the amount of light hitting its surface. The circuits of the camera examine variations in power and map them to specific points on the chip. These data are then turned into photographs. You'll probably hear about two types of chips: CCD

CCD and CMOS sensors

Foveon sensor

(charge-coupled device) and CMOS (complimentary metal oxide semiconductor). The CMOS chips tend to require less power, whereas CCDs have speed advantages, but these differences are becoming smaller and smaller as sensor technologies continue to improve. Both work extremely well. One significant variation of the CMOS chip is the Foveon X3. In all other processors, color is made from special filters that cover individual sensors, and these filters are mixed in a unique pattern that allows a camera to create full color even though each sensor has only one color associated with it. The Foveon chip uses sensors with separate layers for each color. In theory, this should allow cleaner color.

In a digital camera, picture information is stored on a memory card. The more megabytes a card holds, the more images that can be stored before changing cards or transferring the information to the computer or portable hard drive. I recommend a minimum of 256 megabytes (MB), but more are preferable to facilitate shooting birds at the highest

Digital camera sensors mainly work with an array of color filters over different pixels. The full-color image is interpolated from those varied data. A Foveon sensor relies on unique capabilities of silicon to capture complete color information for each pixel.

resolution possible. Lower resolutions and smaller image sizes allow more exposures.

When buying a DSLR camera, select one with the highest number of megapixels you can afford. With more pixels you gain two things: the ability to capture finer detail in a scene, and the capacity to record smoother gradations in tone. Although you may think that sounds like "quality," you cannot see more than a certain amount of detail in any given print size. Extra detail gives no benefit if it does not show up. My 6-megapixel camera generates a file of 17.4 megabytes and, at the printing standard of 300 dots per inch (DPI), allows a top-quality uncropped 8-by-10-inch print. Bumping the print size up to 11-by-14 results in only a slight sacrifice of quality.

It is important to remember that megapixels govern image size, not image quality. A 6-megapixel camera will not necessarily ensure a better 5-by-7-inch print than a 3-megapixel camera, because the 3-megapixel has captured enough detail for the 5-by-7-inch print. However, the leap to a more expensive, higher-end camera with more megapixels also means more versatility—remote-cord capabilities and other improvements. Since the vagaries of bird photography often result in cropping the final image, the larger size is welcome, too.

This basic digital camera process is simple: A light-sensitive sensor turns light energy into electrical impulses. This analog signal is interpreted and translated into image data by a processing chip; the data is then recorded on a memory card.

Image sensor

The digital sensor, except in some of the very high-end DSLRs, is smaller than the 35mm film size. Telephoto lenses, rated for the larger film rather than the smaller sensor, give more magnification. Multiply by 1.5 to determine the gain. A 400mm lens becomes equivalent to a 600mm— a real plus for the bird photographer.

When faster films are needed for 35mm photography, varying amounts of the grain structure of the film become more evident in the print. When you dial in the higher ISO exposure ratings on your digital camera, a similar phenomenon occurs. In the digital world it is referred to as *noise*. Noise also occurs with underexposure and long time exposures.

With all of the pluses of digital photography, are there any negatives? Well, yes. Perhaps most significantly, the cost—not so much the cost of a single camera, but the cost of keeping current with the latest irresistible improvements of a relatively immature technology relative to film. You can also expect that technology changes will force you to scramble at some point to keep your digital archives compatible with the latest hardware and software. In the meantime, keep your files well organized for easy image retrieval, and don't forget to protect your photo files with backups!

TIP

Use the Internet to keep abreast of the fast-changing digital photography industry. A simple keyword query in your area of interest can help you avoid expensive mistakes, such as buying outdated or discontinued items at the local camera store. The Internet will also provide maps and information about an area before you head out.

Analog signal

Digital signal

Image processor

Memory card

256 MEGS MEMORY

USING DIGITAL IN THE FIELD

In the field a well-prepared digital bird photographer should carry at least a medium-sized DSLR kit (including a selection of lenses), with spare batteries and memory cards as well as a battery charger.

The digital SLR (DSLR) in the field presents a few easily solved problems that film cameras don't. First, how many, and what storage-capacity, memory cards do you need to carry? Obviously, the answer depends on the length of time you will be away from the computer where your images will be stored. If you carry a laptop computer in your car or knapsack, you will need fewer cards. There are also an ever increasing number of handheld battery-powered devices to store photographs from the camera or removed memory card. Some units even allow you to burn CDs from the

Waist or hip packs are useful when you are cycling, boating, or hiking because they offer quick and easy access to equipment. Some also offer a protective weather cover for rain.

inserted memory card. Batteries can be charged from your car cigarette lighter or a DC source. DSLRs gobble camera battery power much faster than motor-driven 35mms do, because many more of their functions are battery-dependent. So be sure to carry at least two extra sets in the field. Rather than alkaline batteries, use nickel metal hydride (NiMH) rechargeables or lithium. Some DSLRs use lithium ion rechargeables. The CCD chip is apparently harder on batteries than the CMOS.

When you change lenses, take care to make sure the back element and mount of the lens are free of dust. Point the camera down so as not to collect any dust as you attach the lens. In the field where wind blows and dust abounds, take even more care, especially with zoom lenses. Each speck of dust on the internal CCD or CMOS sensor will appear on the print as a black spot and will have to be removed from the image later, using a computer program such as the cloning tool in Adobe Photoshop. Cleaning the sensor in the field is not an option, since you'll need electricity to lock up the mirror as well as a controlled environment to blow or swab off the CCD surface with delicate tools.

Similar to SLR motor drives, DSLRs can be set to "burst mode" yielding 20 to 30 rapid-fire frames before quitting to allow processing in the camera. This feature makes capturing these flying Herring Gulls easy—assuming the photographer has good enough reflexes.

A disadvantage with DSLRs in the field is inclement weather. Do not get your camera wet! It's full of electronic parts that don't suffer natural elements gladly. I never leave shelter without stuffing a couple of plastic garbage bags in my pockets for emergency waterproof protection.

Often in bright sunshine, all too prevalent in the field, the LCD panel is hard to see well enough to judge whether your exposure is right on. Hoods are available but can be awkward to use quickly. Luckily, high-end DSLRs can bring up clear histograms over the LCD image. Once you learn to read a histogram—very easy—you can see immediately whether your exposure is accurate. Although off exposures can be corrected by the computer to a certain extent, some of the information you should retain in the picture is compromised. If you are used to shooting with older non-automatic lenses on manual settings, you will really appreciate this histogram feature, especially if you're not used to measuring exposure with a handheld meter.

My DSLRs have three shooting modes: single frame, burst mode, and self-timer mode. Burst mode is the closest to an SLR motor drive, but only allows a certain number of frames before the processor kicks in. You will soon find out how many frames per second your DSLR gives you. Since booting-up often takes more time than readying film camera, it is a good idea to keep the camera turned on for the entire session.

My first DSLR, satisfactory for birds in every other way, lacked any provision for attaching a remote cord. Since remote situations do arise in bird photography, I made sure my second purchase could handle a remote, so I wouldn't have to return to film cameras to solve the problem.

Multiple flash presents no more problems than with 35mm. The advantage over 35mm is that you don't need a flash meter or Polaroid to check the lighting. Just look at your LCD panel. All in all, the DSLR is a great tool in the field but does need more tender loving care than a film camera.

—Bates Littlehales

CHAPTER TWO
LURING BIRDS

GETTING CLOSE TO BIRDS

You don't have to travel to faraway and exotic places to photograph birds. You can get started in your own backyard. The main thing is to get close to the birds. (I like a bird to cover at least one third of the width of the picture frame; others might prefer a different proportion.)

You can get close to birds by luring them with food or drink. By putting up the right kinds of feeders and using the right foods, you'll probably be able to attract and photograph many different kinds of birds. A handy table at the back of this book lists the kind of feeders and foods most effective with different birds. Here are the basics you'll need to know.

FEEDERS

In my suburban neighborhood in Rochester, New York, I have been able to attract about 20 different kinds of birds to feeders placed about ten feet from my house. I position the feeders near windows for convenient photography from the comfort of my own home.

While the following text often refers to my experiences in upstate New York, the birds that you will attract will depend on where you live and your specific neighborhood. No matter where you live, you should be able to attract at least a few different kinds of birds using techniques described here.

I use four types of feeders to attract different birds. Three of these hang from fishing line strung between my house and a nearby tree. I use fishing

On a hot day, dripping water attracts a male Indigo Bunting. Better than the garden-variety concrete bird-bath, a natural-looking drip pool will attract more species. Test your skill as a set designer by hanging a water container or dripping hose over the pool.

platform feeder

tube feeder

suet feeder

log feeder

line rather than rope to make it more difficult for squirrels to get to the feeders. Three strands of 40-pound test line do a good job. I originally used a single strand, but it broke too often. Another feeder stays on the ground. I can easily position the feeders at appropriate distances from the window, based upon the size of birds I expect to photograph.

The first of my hanging feeders is a covered platform, which I fill with a variety of seeds—cracked corn, millet, and sunflower seeds. These seeds attract a wide variety of birds in my area, including Northern Cardinals, Black-capped Chickadees, White-breasted Nuthatches, Evening Grosbeaks, Mourning Doves, Common Grackles, Brown-headed Cowbirds, House Finches, and the ubiquitous House Sparrows. Blue Jays also come to this feeder, particularly when I add whole peanuts to the menu. Observe which foods your birds prefer, and feed them accordingly. Keep in mind that prepared bird food mixes often contain seeds that birds don't particularly like.

A nearby suet feeder attracted this male Downy Woodpecker into camera range.

My second hanging feeder is a tube with several small feeding holes and accompanying perches. From this feeder I dispense niger seed, which attracts such birds as American Goldfinches, House Finches, Pine Siskins, and Common Redpolls.

My third feeder is a suet feeder. I use this one only during the cooler months of the year, since suet quickly goes rancid during the hot summer months. I constructed one suet feeder by drilling a one-inch diameter hole in a log and filling it with suet. I hang the log with the hole sideways to the camera, so the suet is not visible from the camera position. On days when I am not taking photographs, I place a much larger quantity of

Sunflower seeds lured this male House Finch. This species stays at the feeder longer than those that grab and go, allowing a close-up taken from a distance such as this. The photographer used an extension tube stacked with a tele-converter.

suet in a wire container attached to the log. Thus, the birds get used to coming and looking for suet at the log, but I don't have to refill the feeder as often. Woodpeckers, nuthatches, and chickadees come to this feeder.

To attract Brown Creepers, I put up a second suet feeder consisting of a wire basket attached directly to a large tree in my backyard. This has successfully lured a few creepers during spring migration. In winter, it also attracts other suet-loving birds.

Finally, I occasionally set up a log feeder on the ground. I hollow out a spot in the top of the log in which to place food. Sometimes I scatter food in the grass in front of the log. I photograph birds at this ground feeder from my basement window.

The birds that come to this feeder include sparrows of various kinds, plus Dark-eyed Juncos, House Finches, Mourning Doves, and Common Grackles; although other birds such as Northern Cardinals, Pine Siskins, Blue Jays, and Black-capped

Chickadees will also occasionally feed on the ground. My best picture-taking opportunities at this ground feeder occur during spring and fall migrations, which bring many temporary visitors, such as White-crowned Sparrows, White-throated Sparrows, Field Sparrows, American Tree Sparrows, Song Sparrows, Pine Siskins, and Dark-eyed Juncos. The juncos often overwinter.

SETTING UP FOR FEEDER SHOTS

To get the best possible picture quality, I avoid shooting through glass windows. Instead, I have made a window insert out of a board in which I have cut an opening for my lens. The opening is as small as possible in order to help keep out cold air during wintry weather. To it, I have attached a piece of imitation leather that fits snugly against my lens.

For the ground feeder, I need a larger opening so that I can vary my distance from the birds, depending on whether they land on the log or on the ground in front of it. This allows me the flexibility to adjust the focus and image size to suit the situation. To minimize cold air coming into the house, I made a booth out of plastic sheeting to surround the window area. I also put up a piece of dark cloth to prevent the birds from seeing me. I avoid quick movements of my lens so as not to frighten the birds.

To achieve a natural look in my photographs, without feeders or other man-made objects showing, I attach branches to the hanging feeders and photograph birds as they land before going to the feeders. For better-looking pictures, I remove bird droppings or other distractions from the branches. I also try to avoid showing a cut or broken end of a branch.

The ground feeder looks natural because the food slot on top is out of camera view. I usually pile some leaves or branches a few feet behind the

TIP
Simplifying your background should be a major consideration in all bird photography. Become aware of visual clutter. Too many distractions go unnoticed until your photographs come back from the processor.

log to serve as an out-of-focus background. The log becomes the background for birds feeding in the grass in front of it.

Depending on where you position your feeders, they will usually receive sunlight only part of the day. With flash, I'm not limited to a couple of hours when the sun is in just the right position. Also, I don't have to worry about clouds and other changeable conditions. Using flash, I can photograph from sunup to sundown.

To get the most natural look possible from my flash photography, I generally use three flash units. I set up the first one as the main light, positioning it slightly above the bird's expected location and to one side at an angle of approximately 45 degrees. The second light is a fill flash aimed at the feeder from the other side of the lens, not far from the camera axis. This flash, set at about one stop less exposure than the main light, helps lighten the shadows. The third light illuminates the background to prevent it from going completely black from underexposure. The extra flash heads are triggered by slaves when they sense light from the flash attached to the camera.

Whenever possible, I use natural foliage as a background. When no suitable natural background is available, I hang a green, brown, or other natural-colored blanket or cloth to serve as an out-of-focus background.

For photography at my feeders, I often use a 450mm lens with extension tubes, the tubes being necessary for closer focusing than my lens normally allows. Be aware of the fact that long-focal-length lenses focused at a close distance have very shallow depths of field (about an inch at the widest aperture of a 450mm f/6.5 lens). This makes careful focusing imperative.

It is easier to obtain a sharp focus across the whole bird when its body lies in a plane perpendicular to your line of sight (a side view). If the pose is something other than this, a smaller aperture may be needed to get the whole bird in focus. To compensate for the smaller aperture, you must use a slower shutter speed that, depending on the film speed, may be too slow to freeze the bird's movement. If the whole bird cannot be brought into focus under the existing circumstances, you should at least make sure that the eyes are in sharp focus.

In taking pictures of birds at feeders, I prefocus my camera on the branch where I expect the bird to land. I usually have to follow up with a last-second adjustment to the focus, depending on the exact position of the bird. Fast action is necessary because the bird usually lands only momentarily on the branch. If you have several feeders, you'll probably have to choose just one each time you set up your flash units for photography. This can be frustrating when an interesting bird comes to a feeder that has not been prepared for photography. But that's all part of the game.

Sometimes a quick change of setup will allow you to get the exact picture you want, and sometimes it will just add to your frustration because

In this setup for photography at feeders (below), a main flash is triggered by a slave. A sync cord attached directly to the camera fires the fill flash, set farther back. A third flash (not shown) illuminates the area behind the bird. The photographer positions the camera lens through a hole in a board placed in an open window and takes pictures of birds as they land on a branch near the feeder.

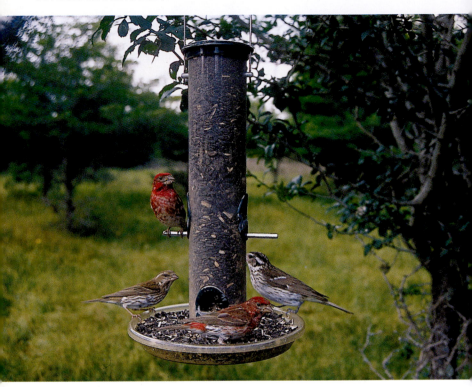

A West Virginia feeder brings in Purple Finches and a female Rose-breasted Grosbeak. The photographer used a remote tripper and a wide-angle lens to give a sense of the surroundings.

different birds alternate visits at the various feeders. Fortunately, most birds will make repeated visits to your feeders.

From time to time, my friends tell me about interesting birds that have shown up at their feeders. I have taken my lighting equipment to their homes and set it up in a similar fashion. I can also take a portable blind to set up about eight to ten feet from the feeder. With this arrangement, I can photograph birds just about anywhere. I have also set up portable bird feeders when I have been traveling. Sometimes I use a small dome tent as an easy-to-assemble blind from which to photograph birds on the ground.

If you have never used a bird feeder before, you will probably be amazed at the variety of birds it will attract. Shortly after setting up my first feeder,

I began seeing bird species in my yard that I'd never seen before. To keep my bird clientele coming back regularly, I make sure to keep my feeders supplied with food.

You don't necessarily have to have a bird feeder in order to attract birds with food. Some birds, such as jays, will take food scraps at picnic areas. In public parks, sometimes wild ducks or other birds look for handouts such as bread and corn. In the winter, when food is scarce, I have fed sunflower seeds to Black-capped Chickadees right from my hand. Make sure to obey local ordinances regarding the feeding of animals.

WINTER PHOTOGRAPHY AT FEEDERS

When winter snows fly, don't put your camera away. You can take lovely pictures of birds such as cardinals, juncos, and chickadees at your feeders in winter.

Think about the kind of scene you want to create. There are lots of possibilities. You can add a cut pine bough to the scene; it will stay fresh-looking for several days in cold weather. Add pine cones, ice, and snow and you have the makings of an artistic masterpiece. After the holidays, you can get all the branches you want from discarded trees. At other times, you should have little difficulty finding a tree from which to trim a small branch.

Berry branches can provide another artistic effect. It's a little harder to get snow to stick to these branches than to those from conifers; one method that works is to spray water on the branch and berries while sprinkling snow over the top. You can place little chunks of snow and ice between the berry stems as well.

Here's one more feeder photography trick. Some birds, chickadees in particular, zip into the feeder and leave so quickly that it is difficult to get good pictures. I have lots of frames of empty branches to prove it!

In a moment of inspiration, I attached a mirror to the feeder. It had the desired result—at least temporarily. When the startled birds first encountered the reflection, they stayed on the branch just long enough for me to get some pictures. It didn't take the chickadees long, however, to figure out that my mirror was no threat. They soon went back to their old ways.

RECORDED BIRD CALLS AND OTHER SOUNDS

Some birds are territorial and will drive intruders away, particularly others of their own species. You can draw some of these birds into close range by playing recordings of their songs. The male bird, thinking an intruder has entered his territory, will

Backyard portraiture: Mourning Dove. Add an extension tube of moderate length to a camera body. Attach a 1.4 tele-extender, then a 300mm lens. Rig your flash setup close enough to the bird's perch on the feeder to stop down to f/16. Sit comfortably in your blind, focus, and shoot. With practice, it's a piece of cake.

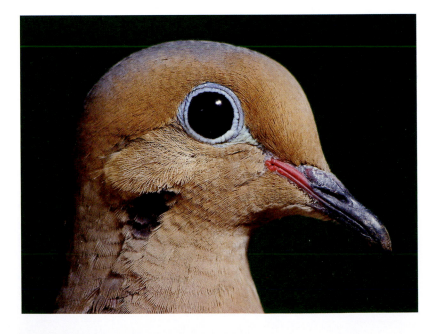

come out to defend it. This technique usually works well only during the nesting season. Use it very sparingly so you don't adversely affect the nesting of the birds.

The first time I tried the tape recording trick, I was amazed at how well it worked. My son, Michael, and I were at a nearby pond. We pulled our van off the road and parked by some cattails. No birds were in sight. I had Michael play the Red-winged Blackbird tape. Immediately, seemingly out of nowhere, a Red-winged Blackbird appeared close to the van.

I have often been able to lure Red-winged Blackbirds to within eight to ten feet of my van—close enough to get full-frame shots using a 450mm lens. I've had a similar experience with a Song Sparrow. You'll find a list of other birds that should respond to bird calls and songs in the back of this book.

Great Horned Owls can be lured into close range with either an actual recording of the bird's call or with a good human imitation of it. Barred and Northern Saw-whet Owls, as well as screech-owls, also respond to recordings. They are best called at night, so you'll need a flash and a helper to shine a light. Playing calls of enemy or prey species also helps to attract birds, which come to hunt or to drive the perceived enemy away. I've found that a screech-owl call works particularly well—you never know what species of birds you might attract.

There are a number of excellent sources for bird songs recorded on CD and tape. Peterson Field Guides and Stokes Field Guides offer collections of bird songs of eastern and western regions of North America. Check your local library for recordings. Catalogs for birding enthusiasts should be a good source, as well.

The best way to use recordings is to copy the ones you want onto your own tape or CD.

TIP

Be aware that on some public lands, the use of tape recorders to lure birds is discouraged or even illegal. Check with the people in charge.

You can make several repeated recordings sequentially on the tape. About five minutes worth of recording for a given bird species should be sufficient.

SQUEAKING AND "SPISHING"

There are two other distinctive sounds that many songbirds will also respond to. You can make a squeaking noise by sucking on the back of your hand. The resulting noise sounds like a bird in distress and can be effective in bringing birds into close range. This technique can be successful in drawing small birds, which are often hiding in bushes, out into the open where they can be photographed.

Making a sound like *spisssh, spisssh, spisssh* (called "spishing") also works. Gray Catbirds respond particularly well to these sounds. Other birds that can be lured closer with squeaking and spishing include Blue Jays, Red-eyed Vireos, Song Sparrows, White-throated Sparrows, Brown Thrashers, Scarlet Tanagers, White-breasted Nuthatches, Blue-gray Gnatcatchers, kinglets, towhees, chickadees, and titmice.

HUMMINGBIRDS

Hummingbirds are attracted to specialized feeders that dispense sugar water through a tube. One part sugar to three parts water makes a good mix.

To get a natural look, I place trumpet-creeper or some other favorite flowers of hummingbirds inside or in front of the feeder opening. When a blossom begins to wilt, I replace it with a fresh one, which I sometimes keep in water or a nearby refrigerator. I crop the picture so the feeder does not show. In some western areas of the United States, thistle flowers are plentiful and easy to use in hummingbird photography. For feeders with multiple openings, I put tape over all but one tube, forcing the birds to come just where I want them.

The first days of spring, before trees have fully leafed out, are ideal for colorful, unobstructed shots, like this one of a Blue Jay approaching a backyard feeder.

Hummingbirds move so fast that it's impossible to know how pictures of them will turn out. Two flash heads set at reduced power to shorten flash duration froze the aerial acrobatics of this female Broad-tailed Hummingbird (above). Natural light doesn't allow a shutter speed fast enough to stop wing action, but the blur of a Ruby-throated Hummingbird's wings doesn't harm this picture (below).

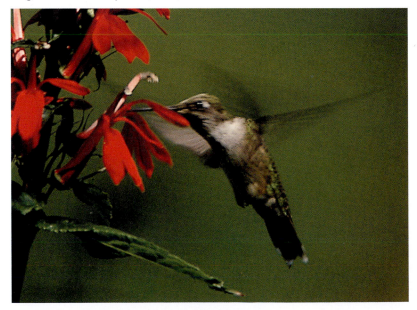

Hummingbirds will habitually return to the same perch time after time. By focusing a long telephoto lens on an observed resting spot and waiting for the bird to return, you can often get good pictures. If you find a bird already sitting on a branch, you may be able to get close to it by moving in very slowly.

■ Flight Photographs

Getting good pictures of hummingbirds in flight is a challenge. Try to photograph them as they hover near the feeder. You will find that you'll probably have a higher failure rate with pictures of hummingbirds than with most other birds. Don't be discouraged— the good shots you get will be very rewarding.

Flash can be a great help in photographing hummingbirds in flight. The flash will help stop the motion of the wings, which move at a rate of about 50 beats per second. Fixed-intensity flash equipment, having a flash duration of around 1/1,000 of a second, will not totally freeze the motion of a hummingbird's wings. Nevertheless, you can take some very nice pictures showing a little wing movement with such flash equipment, or even in sunlight. These pictures will be quite effective as long as the body of the hummingbird looks sharp.

Some flashes have provision for cutting the power down by factors of two (1/2, 1/4, 1/8, 1/16, 1/32 power, etc.). The reduction in power is achieved by a corresponding decrease in flash duration. Using the lowest fractional power practical within the limits of the f-number of the lens and the required depth of field will allow you to reduce or even eliminate the motion of the hummingbird's wings in your photographs.

A word of caution regarding metering exposure for reduced power: Flash meters will often give incorrect readings for fractional power settings

TIP
Make sure you clean hummingbird feeders and replace nectar often, especially in hot weather. Direct sunlight causes food to spoil more quickly, encouraging a deadly mold.

because the flash duration is often too short to activate the meter's measuring circuit.

To get around this problem, meter your flash on full power. Then open up one additional stop for each time the power of the flash is cut in half. Also apply any adjustment necessary if you use extension tubes.

I have found that a 70-300mm zoom lens works quite well, since most hummingbirds will allow a relatively close approach. Such zoom lenses usually have fairly wide apertures and can be quickly adjusted for different-size hummingbirds. Some serious hummingbird photographers build or purchase special flash equipment that gives them flash durations as short as 1/50,000 of a second.

■ Experiment with Backgrounds

Pay attention to the background in your hummingbird photography. If it is sunlit, you may observe "ghosting" around the edges of the bird in your photographs. This often occurs because the shutter is open longer than the duration of the flash, causing a secondary image made by ambient light.

Some photographers hang blue paper behind the bird, making a background that looks like sky. If you use paper, take special care to make sure that it is evenly lit so no shadows from the bird are cast on it. Often, the perfect uniformity of the blue paper looks artificial. I prefer using foliage as a background. Sometimes I use a mottled green background that simulates foliage.

Artificial backgrounds are particularly noticeable when each picture in a set was taken with the same background. I've often noticed that some of the best hummingbird photographers use the same old backgrounds time after time. In a group of pictures, you will sometimes see all sorts of hummingbirds feeding on different flowers, all with the same background. The background would be

TIP

If you travel to a location that caters to hummingbird photographers, consider bringing your own feeders for use in a nearby campground, away from the crowd.

This sequence demonstrates a method devised by author Rulon Simmons for making backgrounds. First, choose a negative from a photograph that has a background you like. Next, make a 16-by-20-inch print of part of the image, out of focus and to the desired hue. Simmons used this leafy background for a Black-chinned Hummingbird (below).

A branch placed to minimize background clutter provides a stopping place for this Dark-eyed Junco and a focal point for the photographer.

wonderful for any individual picture, but seen time and time again in different contexts, it can be annoying to the careful observer.

I found myself in the same trap with my pictures. With just two painted backgrounds, my images were beginning to look an awful lot alike. I painted new backgrounds, but they were nothing great. I could have used plain-colored paper, but I wanted something less artificial-looking.

Then one day an idea hit me. Why not just photograph a background and use a large print as part of my photographic setup? My first thought was to go out and photograph out-of-focus vegetation. (An out-of-focus background will usually compete less for attention than one that is sharply focused.) Then I realized that I didn't even have to shoot additional pictures; I could simply print a portion of sky or vegetation from any number of my existing photographs. The detail doesn't really matter, since just about anything that is printed enough out of focus, particularly if it is a natural-looking color, can work well.

I had been using 16-by-20-inch painted backgrounds, so switching to photographic backgrounds of that standard size was natural. Precise color balancing is not critical. You can use the same negative to make a variety of different backgrounds by choosing different sections, different magnifications, and/or different degrees of focus. You can also vary the color balance and density of the prints to suit your own taste. For example, I have printed fall leaves to a greener color balance than was in the original photograph.

I usually place the background two or three feet behind the bird, approximately the same distance from the bird as the flash units are from the bird on the opposite side. The flashes that illuminate the hummingbirds also light the background. Placing the lights slightly above the birds causes the shadows to fall unseen below the background. Since the background is farther away than the birds, it gets less illumination.

If the background is made at normal density, it will show up slightly darker when photographed with the bird. This usually works fine. If you want a lighter background, it can be printed lighter. Printing on matte paper helps prevent unwanted reflections. The backgrounds can be mounted on cardboard, with paper clips placed through holes in the corners for hanging. I hang the backgrounds from an aluminum frame.

A few additional tricks can add variety to your hummingbird backgrounds. If you plan to use a particular flower in the foreground, try photographing a complementary background ahead of

TIP

When hummingbird nectar comes into contact with feathers, it's destructive. Use a spray water bottle to clean off spilled nectar after filling and rehanging the feeder.

time, incorporating some of the same type of flowers. If you want a simulated sky background, start with a photograph of sky that incorporates some tonal variation so that it doesn't look like just a sheet of blue paper. You can also take a neutral area of any picture and print it extra blue.

With a little creative work in the darkroom, you can make almost any photograph into a suitable hummingbird background. Give it a try with negatives of your own!

BIRDBATHS

Many birds that won't come to a feeder will come to a birdbath. In areas of the western United States where there is still a lot of wild habitat with plenty of natural food, water is often more popular than food for attracting birds. Generally, the drier the surrounding area, the more effective your birdbath will be.

In the eastern United States, where water is plentiful and many natural areas have been replaced with building tracts, bird feeders may be the most effective way to attract birds. But bird-baths still offer lots of opportunities. During migration, a drip pool is a powerful magnet, no matter how wet the climate.

Birds readily come to the sound of dripping water. You can create a drip pool by suspending a garden hose over a birdbath, or make your own device using a plastic soft drink bottle. Fill it with water, tie a string around the neck, and hang it from a branch over the birdbath. Poke a hole in the bottom of the bottle with a small nail, and adjust the cap to control the drip rate.

In winter, birds can have a hard time finding water. You can put out hot water from time to time, or use a bath that heats the water enough to keep it from freezing. For a natural-looking

This Dark-eyed Junco (opposite), fluffing its feathers in a gentle bath, was captured with natural light. The hearty splashing of a Blackburnian Warbler (above) was, in contrast, photographed with an electronic high-speed flash.

Following pages: A Scarlet Tanager cannot be coaxed to a feeder, but it will often come to water. Learn the behavior of the birds you want to photograph, and you'll increase your chances of capturing them on film.

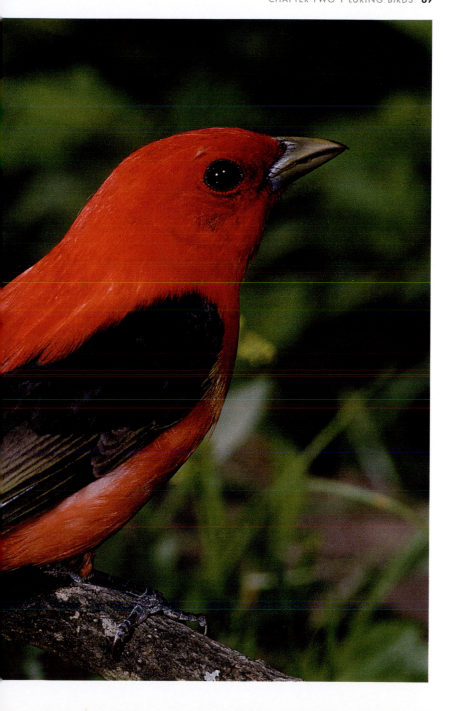

settings, try placing a branch near the birdbath and photograph the birds as they land on it.

SETTING UP A NATURAL-LOOKING POSE

The rules of good composition apply to bird photography. Pay attention to the background for your subject. Try for a background that is not cluttered with distractions. I make a special effort to get a natural look in my photography, eliminating man-made objects such as utility poles, wires, fences, and buildings.

Clutter competes with the subject for attention. Even natural elements, such as a bright and out-of-focus branch, or one that blends into the bird's outline, can be distracting. Try controlling the background by waiting for the bird to move, shifting your position, or luring the bird with food or water to another location.

Working with a long lens often results in shallow depth of field. In the absence of bright, distracting elements, this can help blend the background into a pleasant blur of color.

With the background under control, work with the bird itself. Your job is easy if the bird is at rest. Feeding birds, which are usually in near-constant motion, provide an additional challenge. If your shutter speed won't stop the motion, try making a squeaking sound. This will often cause the bird to stop and stand alert.

Always keep the bird's eye in sharp focus—it's what people usually notice first in a photograph. As the bird moves its head, take your picture when you see a reflection, called the *catchlight*, in its eye.

Complete your composition by careful positioning of the bird within the picture frame. Take care to avoid accidentally clipping off part of the bird's tail or feet, something that's easy to do in a frame-filling shot when you are concentrating on getting sharp focus on its eye.

TIP

Continually focus on the bird's eyes—often the rest will take care of itself. If the eyes are not sharp, you'll be disappointed in your photograph.

Niger seed lured these American Goldfinches to a backyard feeder. Once the birds came to the feeder on a regular basis, the photographer placed a thistle flower next to the feeder. A few niger seeds sprinkled on the thistle blossoms made the perch an instant hit with the goldfinches, providing an excellent natural-looking scene for photographs.

PRINTING DIGITAL

Although the rules of digital printing are standard and can be learned from manuals, an individual has plenty of freedom to be creative within those rules. As a bird photographer, not only will you look at your subject matter differently from other photographers, but you will also look at your prints differently.

From the DSLR camera that gives you (or so you hope) a technically splendid image—well exposed with a good tonal range—you send that image to your computer. The software that comes with your camera will guide you through the transfer. You are now at the point where, in the old days, you had to send a negative or slide to a commercial printer or

A careful use of the exposure and contrast controls in Photoshop allow the printer to register the subtle feather detail of this American Egret. With film the camera exposure needs to be bang-on—not so easy in some light conditions with a white bird.

don your darkroom apron and tackle the printing yourself. To me this was a daunting task. Now the computer removes that step and the waiting time entirely. Once the image is stored in the computer, the fun begins. You are about to give your bird a new life.

Instead of listing all of your options in preparing your image and sending it to the desktop printer, I'll describe my own approach. You'll develop yours as you go if you haven't already done so. I recommend that you read not only manuals and books but also magazine articles, which are often full of hints and shortcuts. You should also expect to waste paper and inks as you perfect your printing.

From the DOCK on my Mac's computer monitor, I open the latest version of Adobe Photoshop (one of many programs on the market). Next, under FILE, I scroll down to OPEN. This brings up the storage file containing the bird picture I want to print. I highlight the file name and click twice to open the picture on the monitor screen.

Since I chose to shoot at the highest resolution to preserve the most information possible and also to create a larger megabyte file, the picture opens that way on the screen. Hmm. It doesn't look so bad. Photoshop has extrapolated the information and made some automatic corrections so it looks as if I'm in the ballpark. The exposure, however, is not quite what I want, so I move a bar slider to the left, slightly darkening the image to match my idea of how the bird's plumage should look. I can do this with other bars for tint, temperature, brightness, contrast, shadows, etc. I even have a histogram to remind me to avoid extremes of darks and lights.

When the image looks okay, I click on OPEN. A new image comes to the screen in Photoshop. Now I can make small corrections with a choice of tools. I can put my decision making to the test. Is this area too light or dark for the rest of the image?

A monitor-calibration system—composed of a hardware colorimeter (left) and its accompanying software—provides you with much greater accuracy and control than your computer's built-in utility, which relies on strictly eyeball measurements.

A useful tool in Photoshop is the Unsharp Mask filter (opposite), found under the Filter menu. This window allows you to control the softness or sharpness of an image. Try toggling on and off the preview button to see if the settings you've chosen produce the desired effect.

Would a touch more contrast help or hurt the statement? If I use the saturation tool will the bird look too garish? How much sharpening with the Unsharp Mask filter is enough or too much? Did I remove all the dust the last time I cleaned my sensor, or do I need to remove that tiny black speck on the image with the cloning tool?

Having recently calibrated my monitor to industry standards, I have confidence my screen image will be a reasonable approximation of the final print. The image is never an exact match, because monitors handle light differently than inked paper does. Since Photoshop can communicate with my printer, I chose my settings under FILE, load paper, and then tell it to print. The printer hums away for a few minutes, then ejects the finished print. I never cease to be impressed.

To print a film transparency or negative digitally, you must first scan it—or have it scanned at a shop that offers that service. Once it has been scanned and uploaded into Photoshop, the steps for printing are the same.

—BATES LITTLEHALES

CHAPTER THREE

STALKING BIRDS

IN PURSUIT OF BIRDS

With some care and patience, you can stalk quite a number of birds successfully with a camera. Some species, of course, are more approachable than others. Birds of a species found in one locality may be more approachable than birds of the same species in a different place.

Birds on public beaches, in parks, refuges, and other areas where they are used to seeing people will often be more habituated and more approachable than similar birds in other locations. Zoos with outdoor exhibits often attract a variety of wild birds that can be photographed quite easily. For example, I once took a picture of a very tame Northern Mockingbird at the National Zoo in Washington, D.C., using only a 70-210mm zoom lens.

Obviously, the tamer the bird, the easier it will be to stalk. Some birds known for their tameness include: Gray Catbirds, Spruce Grouse, Gray Jays, Saw-whet Owls, White-tailed Ptarmigans, Least Sandpipers, Black-capped Chickadees, Pine Grosbeaks, kinglets, and dowitchers.

The Grasshopper Sparrow returned to this singing perch after making his territorial rounds. A 600mm lens allowed the photographer to shoot from just outside the sparrow's flight distance—the amount of space he needed to feel secure.

■ Ways to Approach Wary Birds

There are ways to bring home good pictures of wary birds, too, if you follow some basic guidelines. First, take your time when you approach your subject. Move slowly, pretending not to be too interested in the bird.

Take an indirect path toward the bird. Do not stare—it could be seen as threatening. Look in

another direction as much as possible, with only occasional glances toward the creature of interest.

Move toward the bird a short distance at a time, stopping now and then to let it become accustomed to your presence. It will help if you move when the bird is looking away from you. Crouching down can help because it minimizes your profile; this usually makes you appear less threatening.

■ Shoulder Stocks

Wherever practical in bird photography, I use a tripod, which can hold the camera and a long lens rock steady in the field. But shoulder stock mounts developed for cameras work well for stalking birds.

A shoulder stock will come in very handy for photographing birds in flight with a long lens. Be sure to use film that is fast enough to minimize any blurring of the image that might occur due to camera movement.

Brace the shoulder stock against a tree or some other firm object to reduce motion. If no such

TIP
Try building a floating blind so that you can stalk shorebirds from the water. The different perspective can produce excellent results.

The photographer used a 600mm lens to capture this intimate portrait of a Spectacled Eider in a captive waterfowl collection.

object is handy, shooting from a kneeling position helps. If you have a shoulder strap you can tighten it with pressure from your arm; this will also help reduce movement of the lens. An image-stabilizing lens, if you can afford one, also makes stalking easier, eliminating the need for tripods or shoulder stocks in many situations.

LIGHTING CONDITIONS

Before going stalking, think about where the sun will be relative to you and your subjects. For example, if you are photographing birds along the west shore of a north-south running shoreline, you will want to photograph in the afternoon rather than the morning to get good front-lighted subjects.

Full sun can help bring out the brilliant colors of a bird and provide good contrast in the ratio of lights to darks in a picture. Hazy sunlight, or even the flat lighting of a cloudy day, may occasionally be desirable for white birds such as gulls.

A boat did the stalking of this pair of Whooping Cranes while the photographer handheld a 600mm lens comfortably on deck. A tripod would have conducted vibrations to the camera.

White birds usually contrast sufficiently with their surroundings, even under overcast conditions. But in full sunlight, there is often too much contrast between the white feathers and dark feathers or other dark areas of the picture. In these cases, the whites will either look washed out or the dark areas will lack detail, depending on how you set the overall exposure.

SHOREBIRDS

Many shorebirds lend themselves to stalking, particularly if they are along a shoreline rather than in a large open field or mudflat. These birds are often quite intent on feeding, so if you approach cautiously, you should be able to get close to them.

While shorebirds are feeding, they are typically in constant motion, probing in the mud or sand for food. Don't pass up the opportunity to get some behavioral shots of the birds feeding in their habitat. The action can make for interesting pictures.

Desert birds like this House Finch seem tamer and easier to stalk than birds in other locations, perhaps because so few humans and pets visit this inhospitable place.

■ Getting a Bird's Attention

Birds in motion can be difficult to photograph at times, particularly if your equipment and lighting conditions require using slower shutter speeds. You may also have difficulty keeping the camera focused on a moving bird (particularly with manual focus). As already mentioned, in such situations a useful technique is to get the bird's attention by making a quick noise, which will usually cause your subject to stop and stand alert, at least momentarily.

However, if you make the same sound too many times, the bird will learn to ignore it. When this happens, try making a different noise. If your camera has a motor drive, the sound of film advancing after the first shot will often elicit an alert expression from the bird.

TIP

You can easily sink down into a mudflat in pursuit of shorebirds. Try walking in snow shoes across the unstable goop.

If a bird has become accustomed to your being nearby, sometimes making a quick movement with your hand will cause it to pause. If you try this with a bird before it has grown comfortable with your presence, though, there is a good chance that it will fly away before you have had a chance to take any photographs.

Fortunately, when a shorebird flies, it often doesn't go very far. You may be able to follow along the water's edge and try again in a few minutes. If the shorebirds haven't flown too far away, be patient. Waiting for them to come closer to you will often pay off.

Sometimes you will be able to approach a bird undetected by hiding behind an object such as a dirt bank, a shrub, or tall grass. It's usually difficult

Tundra Swans landed in an inlet as the photographer sat quietly on the bank, not even attempting concealment. Backlighting, as in this photo, demands careful metering for proper exposure.

to get close enough to make good pictures without being seen at all. Move slowly and quietly so that if the bird does see you, you won't appear to be threatening to it.

A trick that sometimes works with flocks of birds, such as gulls, is to "herd" them. To do this, position yourself as close to the birds as they will allow. Wait a few minutes to let them become accustomed to your presence. Then have a helper come slowly toward you from the other side of the flock. The birds will generally move away from your helper and nearer to you. When they do, be ready.

When you're stalking birds on public beaches, there is always the chance that other people will come along and frighten the birds away. To help avoid such problems, go to the beach early in the day, before many people have arrived. It also can be helpful to have someone with you who can try to steer other people away from the area where you are taking photographs.

When you're photographing along the shore, it's possible to have too much of a good thing: Getting a group of birds in good overall focus means dealing with a depth of field problem that can present quite a challenge. Sometimes it will be best to just focus on one or two birds at a time.

Besides beaches, other good places to photograph shorebirds are along breakwaters, brackish

Following spread: Sanderlings feed on a winter beach at sunrise. In this case, the challenge was leaving a cozy bed in the cold and dark to arrive in time for dawn.

Shorebirds, absorbed with hunting for bits of food, lend themselves to stalking. The trick is to convey their characteristic motion in a still photograph. Above, from left to right: Willet, Black-bellied Plover, and Lesser Yellowlegs. Below: Long-billed Dowitchers.

ponds, and inlets. Each of these locations will give you excellent opportunities to explore the world of birds.

A male Barrow's Goldeneye takes the plunge. The split-second timing demands a sports photography approach, familiarity with bird behavior, and, of course, luck.

DIVING BIRDS

For taking photographs of diving birds such as grebes, loons, and some ducks, the following technique often works well. Stand still while the bird is on the surface. When the bird dives, quickly run to the point on the shore nearest to where you expect the bird to surface. By watching its diving and surfacing pattern, you can usually get a good idea of the direction in which the bird will swim and about how far.

When the diving bird surfaces, make sure you are still and ready to shoot. Prefocus your camera near the spot where you expect the bird to surface. When the bird surfaces, quickly fine-tune the focus and shoot. The bird will usually accept your presence, provided you don't make any rapid movements, but don't expect it to remain on the surface for long. It's often easier to stalk diving birds when they are swimming in relatively narrow bodies of water, such as channels or streams.

SONGBIRDS

Stalking songbirds is generally easier in the spring before the trees and bushes are fully leafed out. Fortunately, this is also the time when birds migrate through to their breeding grounds and are decked out in their finest plumages. Birds are also singing at this time, making them particularly easy to find. Learn to recognize their songs, and you'll know what birds are in the area before you can see them.

Songbirds like to sing from high vantage points such as the tops of trees or bushes. Take note of the locations that birds use for singing, and position yourself near one. Then wait quietly for the bird to return. When birds are feeding on naturally occurring fruits, berries, and seeds, they will often ignore your presence if you approach slowly and work quietly.

Hunkered down on the bank of a wetland area, the photographer caught the reflection of a Great Egret behind a female Northern Shoveller. Stalking gives you the leeway to move the camera and better relate the foreground to the background.

REMAINING UNSEEN

Some techniques discussed in this book require hiding from birds. This is usually best accomplished with a blind. Blinds are useful at nests, feeders, or any other areas regularly visited by birds. They may be portable, for use in the field, or permanent, as found at some wildlife refuges. Sometimes, even your car or home can serve as a good blind.

A makeshift blind can be made from natural materials such as branches or reeds. As you become more involved in bird photography, you may want to construct a portable blind. The diagram on page 93 illustrates an easy-to-make blind using inexpensive PVC tubing, bungee cords, and fabric. Burlap is frame-covering fabric that allows air to pass through, but in strong backlight it reveals the

This camouflaged dome-style tent makes an excellent blind for photographing birds in open spaces.

photographer's form inside. Camouflage cloth is an excellent option.

Small dome tents, which are particularly easy to assemble, make effective blinds for birds on or near the ground. A refrigerator carton can be transformed into a temporary blind, but you'll have to make a few holes for ventilation as well as for your lens.

It helps to make the blind blend as much as possible into the natural surroundings. For this reason, greens and browns are usually the preferred colors. For particularly wary birds, covering the blind with branches or other natural vegetation may also be necessary.

Another simple and effective method of hiding is to sit quietly under camouflage netting. The netting is easy to use and allows good air circulation. If you have to move, do so preferably when birds are not present. Otherwise move as slowly as possible so you don't attract the attention of the birds.

When you position your blind, keep in mind the lighting direction and how the light will change while you are in the blind. Also consider the most likely flight path of your subject and where the bird will land.

The great benefit of a blind is to put the photographer closer to the birds, such as these Canada Geese, without frightening them into flying away.

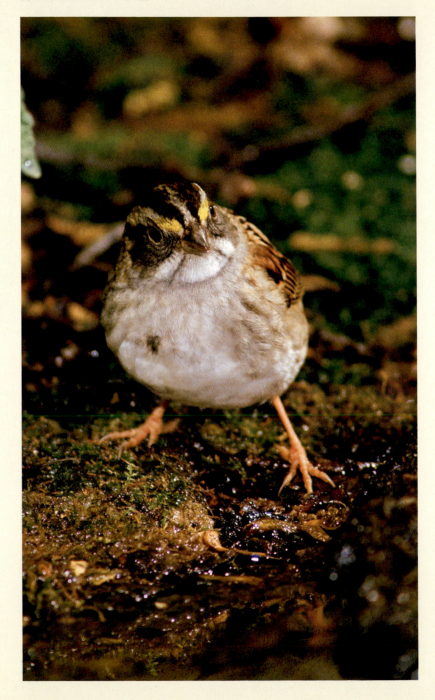

Whenever possible, enter and leave blinds when birds are not present, thus minimizing disturbance. For long stays in a blind, take a stool or chair and anything else that will make your time there as comfortable as possible. You could be waiting a while, so consider taking a good book to read.

At times, the best blind of all may be your car. Birds seem less afraid of cars than of people on foot, and will often allow vehicles to get fairly close. Approach slowly, without making sudden moves. When you're in a good position, you can turn the car engine off.

When I take photographs from my car window, I occasionally place a piece of cloth over the window to hide behind. Even that is usually unnecessary, as long as I don't make any quick movements.

Many wildlife refuges are particularly well suited to photographing birds from a car. They often have roads that loop around ponds and other bodies of water where you can find birds feeding, particularly in the early morning and late afternoon hours.

Birds on the ground and in trees, particularly along wildlife refuge roadways, are often fairly easy subjects to photograph from a car. If you drive up slowly while a bird is feeding, it will often continue without much concern. If it does fly away, be patient—it may return in a few minutes to get back to work.

A beanbag or even a folded jacket makes a good window rest for a long lens and will help absorb vibrations. Manual windows, if your car has them, work best, since they can be slowly raised and lowered at any time, even when your car engine is off.

As you can see, many options exist for blinds. Choose one that meets your needs, and you'll soon be very close to birds.

—RULON E. SIMMONS

A lightweight camouflage net (above) makes an instant blind when draped over the photographer. Always avoid any quick motion that could frighten birds.

A wintering White-throated Sparrow (opposite) was an easy mark from a backyard blind. A good trick when you're using flash on a shot like this is to light the area—not just the moving bird.

BUILDING BLINDS

The perfect portable blind does not exist commercially. Some come close, but are expensive. This design can be modified with little trouble. For floating, it can even be customized to fit an inner tube. Peepholes and camera ports can be sized to suit the photographer and equipment.

For your backyard blind, use two 132-inch lengths of 1-1/4-inch-diameter PVC flexible tubing. For easier portability, use four 66-inch lengths and two wooden dowels that match the inner diameter. Cement one end of each dowel into one end of a 66-inch length, then put the two 66-inch lengths together on the work site and tape the joints. Heavy, long nails will work as well as tent pegs.

Light cotton camouflage cloth, which usually comes in a 44-inch width, makes excellent cover, and camouflage netting can cover the peephole or holes. Cotton is lightweight for carrying long distances, is breathable, and doesn't show the photographer's silhouette when backlit. Drape the uncut cloth over the assembled blind frame and use chalk to draw the shape. Cut four arc-shaped pieces. Sew together except for the entrance, which will close from inside with Velcro.

—Bates Littlehales

Left to right: duct tape, four tent pegs, two 132-inch lengths of 1-1/4-inch-diameter PVC tubes, four bungee cords.

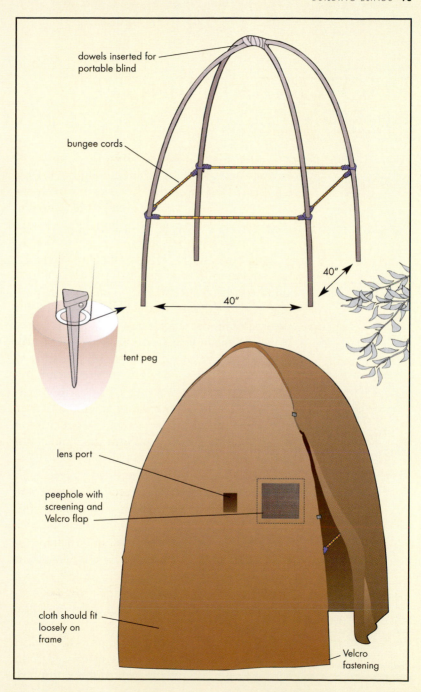

dowels inserted for portable blind

bungee cords

40"

40"

tent peg

lens port

peephole with screening and Velcro flap

cloth should fit loosely on frame

Velcro fastening

CHAPTER FOUR

PHOTOGRAPHING NESTING

PHOTOGRAPHY AT NESTS

Taking photographs of birds at their nests usually requires setting up a blind. There are, however, some situations that can make getting these pictures easier and don't require a blind. First, let's take a look at some of these cases.

Some birds, such as Killdeers and Horned Larks, nest on the ground and will often stay on their nests when approached. A friend of mine once photographed a Killdeer that had built a nest near the parking lot of a large company. When people came to work in the morning, they walked right past the bird, which stayed on its nest. My friend took advantage of the opportunity to photograph this cooperative subject.

Years later, I had a similar opportunity to photograph a nesting Killdeer in another backyard. A friend had taken photographs of the bird at close range with a 50mm lens.

I figured it would be easy to photograph this Killdeer. I armed myself with my 70-210mm zoom lens and marched right up to the nest with my curious children trailing behind me.

This, of course, proved to be too much for the bird, which took off from its nest and flew a short distance away. There it feigned a broken wing, a trick often used by Killdeer to lure predators away from their nests. Unfortunately, I couldn't get near the bird that day.

The next day I returned and proceeded more cautiously. Pretending not to be interested in the bird, I slowly and quietly walked to a point near

When the photographer added a natural-looking log façade to an existing entrance for a nesting box, the female Eastern Bluebird readily accepted this change to its living quarters.

Killdeers will tell photographers and predators they are too close by doing the wounded-bird act (top) to lead them away from their nests. Most plovers, and also some other ground-nesting birds, exhibit this behavior. The precocial Killdeer chick (bottom), never far from its protective parent, relies on cryptic coloration for camouflage.

enough to get good shots with my 450mm lens. I was able to get some good pictures in this way without a blind. Soon, the bird seemed to get used to my presence. A few times it flew from the nest, but it always returned, even when I stood nearby.

Though I meant no harm in my attempts to photograph this nesting bird, I have since learned to avoid doing things that might push a bird to leave its nest while it's sitting on eggs. Doing its broken-wing act, the Killdeer expended a lot of energy—energy needed for warming eggs. Try to avoid any disruptions that might endanger the birds you're photographing.

NESTING BOXES

Photographing birds at their nesting boxes can be relatively easy. I've photographed Tree Swallows and Eastern Bluebirds this way. My first experience photographing at a nesting box was with a pair of Tree Swallows that had moved into a box that my son had put up as part of an Eagle Scout project.

To get a natural-looking picture, I cut a slab off a log and nailed the flat side to the front of the box as a façade. I cut a hole to correspond to the original opening in the bird box.

The birds seemed puzzled when they first saw the modification to their house, but within ten minutes they were flying in and out of it again. I set up a flash near the box and photographed the birds from about ten feet away, using a 600mm lens. I even took some pictures at closer range with my 70-210mm zoom lens.

The following year, I used the same façade on a different box for photographing bluebirds. In photographing Tree Swallows and bluebirds, I put a blanket over my head to hide myself from the birds. I soon found that this wasn't necessary—at least in the case of the Tree Swallows.

TIP

A nesting box or cavity can be used to take action shots by remote control as the bird leaves the hole. Prefocus, then start your motor drive when the bird's head emerges.

SEABIRD COLONIES

Colonies of seabirds can offer many interesting opportunities for photographs at nesting time, but before you set out for these sites, it's wise to check with local wildlife authorities to find out the best and least disruptive time to take photographs. Many such nesting areas are on islands accessible only by boat—and even boats have to keep their distance.

Some nesting colonies suffer badly from visits from humans and their pets. Eggs and young can be harmed by the sun when their parents fly off the nest in fright. Predatory gulls seize such opportunities to devour the eggs or young birds.

FINDING NESTS

Now that we have discussed some of the easier situations for photography at nests, let's look at more typical—and more challenging—situations. First, you have to locate a nest. This usually requires a good pair of binoculars, careful observation, and patience.

A nesting box with its face cut from a log provides a natural-looking backdrop for photography.

Friends can also provide useful leads. It is a big help if the nest is conveniently located, but many are not. The persistent photographer may have to build a scaffold to the proper height for picture taking. Whether or not a scaffold is necessary, you'll probably need a blind.

When possible, it's best to build a blind over a period of time so that the change in the birds' environment will not be too abrupt. As an alternative, you can construct a blind at some distance from the nest and then gradually move closer. This starting point should be beyond the flushing distance of the bird.

With small birds like warblers, it may take as much as a day to move the blind into position and get it ready for photography. With larger birds like hawks and herons, it may take a week or more. A fake camera and flash can also be positioned to get the birds used to the intrusion before you begin to take pictures.

As you make each change, back off and observe the parent birds' behavior through binoculars to make sure that the birds will return to the nest. A trick that can be very successful in photography at nests is to have a "go awayster." This is a person who accompanies the photographer to the blind, but then leaves, making enough noise so that the birds take notice of the exit.

Most birds are believed to be unable to count. When one person leaves, the birds think no one is left in the blind, so they return to the nest much sooner. For this trick to continue to work, the bird must not recognize that it has been tricked. In order to maintain the deception, the "go awayster"

This nest of California Gulls, with newly hatched chicks, was photographed from a portable blind a safe distance from the action. Working this way, you can wait for telling gestures that add to the interest of the image.

TIP

Don't be in a hurry to tackle nest photography—it takes preparation and expertise. People who have been the least intrusive—and most successful— have studied for years.

must return to retrieve you. A handkerchief or a cell phone call can signal the helper to return.

REMOTE PHOTOGRAPHY

Another technique for photographing nesting birds is to position your camera close to the nest while positioning yourself some distance away with a remote release. In some cases, you may find that you will need to conceal yourself as well as you can.

Remote photography will allow you to take pictures of birds with minimal disturbance to them. From a distance, you can activate the shutter by means of a mechanical shutter release, a wired electrical release, or a radio-controlled release.

Cameras with automatic film advance are desirable for such photography, since they minimize disturbance of the birds. They also provide for uninterrupted opportunities to take pictures.

A larger-format camera can be useful for remote photography. It is difficult to frame a tight 35mm shot, since the exact position the bird will take is somewhat unpredictable. The larger image area permits cropping after the picture is taken.

Unpredictability of the bird's position can also lead to focus problems. Observe the bird's behavior before setting up the camera so you'll be able to anticipate what will happen. Those who relate to the bird have the best chance of success when adjusting the camera focus.

USING FLASH

You can get away from problems created by variable natural lighting by using flash. If lighting conditions are changeable, an automatic exposure control will also be necessary. Nests are usually found in shaded areas of vegetation where flash may be required anyway.

When you set up your flash units, place one flash as a main light source somewhat above the nest. Angle the light to make the bird's shadow

The photographer visited these Snow Geese nests with an ornithologist, who weighed and tagged goslings while the parent geese waited nearby. The birds were quickly photographed, then left alone.

Following pages:
To get this image, the photographer spent days in a tent blind watching a TV monitor that was wired to a videocam high in a pine tree near the Bald Eagle nest. When the adult showed up on the screen, the photographer punched a button, which fired a motor-driven still camera mounted by the videocam. The bird's widely spaced nest visits made for tedious days that started early and ended late. The photographer had to enter and exit the blind in pitch darkness; sharp-eyed eagles are not tolerant beings.

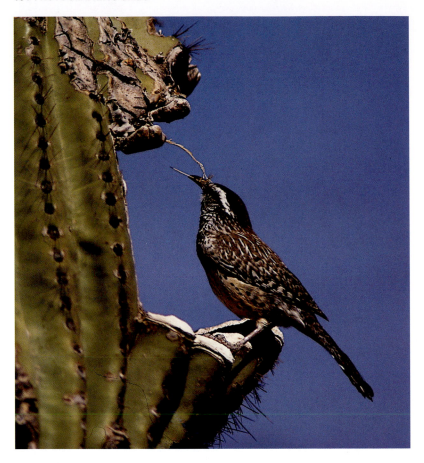

Cactus Wrens build one false nest after another, giving the photographer plenty of opportunity to catch them in the act.

fall low so that it does not hit the vegetation directly behind the bird and create a dark shaow in the image.

A weaker flash with about one stop less exposure, when used as fill flash, can lighten shadowed areas on the bird. Sometimes you'll need a light on the background as well to keep the background from going too dark.

THE WELL-BEING OF BIRDS

Whenever you are taking photographs, be particularly conscious of the birds' welfare, avoiding any unnecessary disturbance. At times, this may require backing off and missing a picture, but there will be other opportunities. Don't just march up to bird nests the way I once did and start taking photographs.

You should approach the birds in a way that doesn't startle or alarm them. This means approaching them slowly and sometimes retreating, giving them plenty of time to get used to your presence in the area without feeling threatened. As previously mentioned, with some birds this may mean setting up a blind at some distance from a nest and gradually moving it closer over a period of several days. If possible, enter and leave your blind when both parent birds are away from the nest.

With today's ubiquitous use of cell phones, consider having a friend observe conditions nonintrusively from a distance and report over the phone when it is safe to leave the blind. If necessary, this person can also come to retrieve you, as discussed earlier in this chapter.

Do some research before you set out with your camera. Talk to wildlife experts—refuge managers or biologists—about the least intrusive ways to photograph nesting birds and the best times for it. Also make your own observations from a distance before beginning your photography. Predetermine the birds' feeding schedule and regularity so that you will know if your presence is disturbing them.

Where practical, use a telephoto lens to help maintain a more comfortable distance from nesting birds. When artificial lighting is needed, you can use wirelessly triggered remote flashes placed closer to the nest.

■ Altricial Birds

For altricial birds, those born without feathers, it is safest to wait for at least five days after the young have hatched before you begin to take pictures.

TIP

Unlike birding, bird photography is a solitary business. Resist human companionship in the field and concentrate on relating to the bird.

There's no need to rush: There will still be plenty of time to take photos as the parents feed their young.

After the young have hatched, parent birds have strong instincts that draw them to their young. You can set up a blind earlier, but birds may abandon their nest if you begin to photograph too soon. Once the young birds get close to fledging age, photography should be terminated so as not to cause premature fledging.

■ Precocial Birds

My strategy is a little different with precocial birds, which are born with down and leave the nest within a few hours of hatching to learn to feed themselves. Photography has to begin somewhat earlier. Even so, the blind should not be set up until the parent birds have been incubating for at least a week.

■ Tread Lightly

Even careful photographers can cause nesting failure in their attempts to get good pictures. Predators, for example, will sometimes follow the photographer's trail of trampled grass right up to the nest.

To help ensure the birds' well-being, there are other cautions to observe. Never cut away branches to expose a nest. Most birds take great care in hiding their nests from potential predators. In gaining access for photography, make little or no adjustments to the area. Never compromise the birds' safety by exposing the nest to either direct sunlight or the view of predators. Make sure that the birds accept your equipment in the vicinity of their nest. Try to set up your equipment when the parent birds are away. This will require working quickly and perhaps positioning various items over a period of time. Getting a photograph you were after isn't worth endangering the subjects you love.

You'll have plenty of chances to take great photographs of birds without putting either of you in jeopardy.

The photographer stood on a cliff to get this image of a nesting colony of Common Murres and Pelagic Cormorants on an island off the California coast, stopping down his telephoto lens to keep the scene in focus.

COURTSHIP

Courtship, which often begins before or during migration and continues into nesting, gives the photographer an opportunity to make some of the most interesting images in the bird year.

The length birds go to in order to say "look at me" and "this territory is mine" is amazing. Not all songbirds sing before reaching the nesting grounds, but enough of them do to fill the leafing trees with sound—almost as if they are warming up for the really serious singing ahead.

When the males arrive at their final destination, they use song to warn away other males and to

A male Greater Prairie Chicken (below) struts and booms early in the morning on a traditional courting ground. Inflated throat sacs make a center of interest in the photo. A male Red-winged Blackbird (opposite) proclaims his territory with a croaky song and flash of bright epaulets.

The male Ruddy Duck slaps his bill against his breast, bubbling the water in front of him in his courtship display. More difficult to capture on film was his surprising rush across the water (below) to impress the female.

attract females. Often they will return to the same series of singing perches—good places to set up portable photo blinds or do some quiet stalking. Bursts of song not only animate the birds, but are often accompanied by behavioral display antics that impress photographers as well as other birds.

The plumage of male songbirds is often the finest feathery color for courtship. The Scarlet Tanager, for instance, changes from dull winter yellow to brilliant red and wows the female, still feathered in yellow-green. In some birds, unfeathered skin parts can also change color. The Great Egret, for example, shows green facial skin next to its bill only during courting season.

The Gray Jay's courtship might be more subtle than that of many other species of birds, but it is still very photogenic. Look for pair bonding in other seasons as well.

Some birds posture, strut, and dance in ways that have long captivated humans as well as other birds. Some Native American dances were based on the strutting of prairie chickens. The bowing and curtsying of European society is also likely based on the behavior of birds.

Courtship is ritualized, and in nesting colonies, prescribed behavior quickly identifies the flying-in bird to the sitting bird. The greeting ceremony provides good photographic opportunities, as long as the photographer keeps a reasonable distance from the birds and uses lenses with long focal lengths. Photo blinds placed at a safe distance will increase your chances of getting good pictures.

There are too many horror stories about photographers disturbing nesting colonies. Imagine the damage a frisky pet brought along by its master can do in one romp through a colony of ground-nesting terns. Enemies such as heat, cold, and marauding gulls take enough toll without any help from humans.

There's so much to photograph in this magic time. Awareness of the birds' well-being will only increase your enjoyment.

—BATES LITTLEHALES

These antics (right), part of the greeting ceremony at a Great Blue Heron's nest, reassure the sitting bird that the flying-in bird is indeed the same mate that flew out. Shooting from across a pond, the photographer caused no impact on the nesting colony.

The elaborate courtship ritual of Northern Gannets (opposite) includes birds raising their bills high in the air. At large nesting colonies, plenty of opportunities exist for making courtship images. These birds allowed the photographer to get close enough to use a 70-300mm zoom lens.

CHAPTER FIVE

PHOTOGRAPHING FLIGHT

THE WONDERS OF FLIGHT

Who hasn't marveled at the graceful flight of a bird? Capturing this grace in photographs is perhaps the most challenging and rewarding aspect of bird photography.

My earliest successful attempt at photographing birds in flight took place on a boat returning from a trip to the island of Martha's Vineyard, just off the coast of Massachusetts. People on the boat began offering food to Herring Gulls, and soon a number of the birds were hovering just overhead. This provided an excellent opportunity to photograph them while they were nearly stationary.

The slow motion of these birds was important to my success, since at that time my photographic equipment was quite limited; I simply used a manual-focus 100mm lens. As the gulls hovered above, I could easily focus on them. Had they been flying by at full speed, focusing would have been very difficult, if not impossible, for me.

My friend Brian Keelan has used another trick for getting successful pictures of birds in flight. His method works well with cameras that have motorized film advance. He makes a through-focus series of photographs—continually changing focus as he shoots pictures of a passing bird. This technique uses a lot of film, but it usually produces one or two good images when the focus is just right.

AUTOFOCUS LENSES

In recent years, autofocus equipment has become popular with photographers. What a difference

Like calligraphic writing against a simple background, a flock of geese silhouetted across the sky makes a dramatic statement.

The photographer used an autofocus 70-300mm zoom lens to capture this Mallard in flight. For an overhead shot of a bird in flight, there is little time to frame the bird.

it can make in flight photography! When I bought my first autofocus camera and lens, a whole new world of bird photography suddenly opened up to me.

Most manufacturers produce autofocus lenses with camera systems designed around them. With autofocus, be sure to check your manual to learn the different focus modes. The most common mode is to focus on the center of the frame. As a bird approaches, establish the focus by pushing the shutter release part of the way down.

One of the drawbacks of autofocus lenses is that if the bird is extremely out of focus at first, the lens may have a hard time determining the correct direction in which to drive the focus. I try to have the camera prefocused at the approximate distance at which I expect to pick up the bird in my viewfinder.

Once your camera is focused, you will have to keep the shutter release partially depressed to maintain the focus as the bird continues to move. Some advanced autofocus lenses will actually predict the proper change in focus based on the relative motion of the bird and the camera.

GETTING STARTED

Once you have a good handle on how to use your autofocus, you are ready to give flight photography a serious try.

I suggest starting with easy birds, such as gulls. Take a helper with a loaf of bread to a nearby beach or garbage dump. Ever watchful gulls will come immediately when your helper holds up a piece of bread. Your biggest problem may be singling out one bird.

Even if you don't have an autofocus lens, you should be able to get some pictures of these birds. If you live in Florida or another location inhabited by Brown Pelicans, you may be able to find a bridge or boat harbor where passing pelicans can be photographed at fairly close range.

Photographing waterfowl in flight is generally a step up in difficulty compared to the situations just described. With patience, you can wait concealed in a blind for a passing duck or goose to come in close.

A large bay in Rochester, New York, partially freezes during most winters. Good numbers of ducks concentrate there, mostly Mallards, in small open pools near the shore. I've found that I can lure these ducks out of the water with cracked corn.

My wife, Rebecca, helps by scattering corn at the upper end of the boat ramp while I wait near the water's edge as the ducks march by. I then step onto the ramp, cutting off the ducks' ground path back to the water. As I move toward the ducks, they take to the air to return to the water,

TIP

As in real estate, it's location, location, location for flight shots with a decent background. Aim for good light direction, room to swing the camera, and, above all, the location that will provide the most chances for finding the most birds.

Following pages: Panning with this close-flying American Avocet was reactive, not planned. The focus was on the bird before it left the water, so there was no need to refocus in flight.

Sky backgrounds often fool a camera's metering system into under-exposing the subject. This Arctic Tern was photographed using an exposure reading taken off an object on the ground with average reflectance. When metering directly off a bird in a blue sky, try-giving an additional 1/3 to 1/2 stop exposure to properly expose the bird. Give one or two stops additional exposure when the sky is white.

giving me an opportunity for close-up flight shots as they go by.

A nice thing about flight photography is that it gives you another option that may allow you to get pictures of a species that would otherwise be very difficult to photograph. Once, on a trip to the Dry Tortugas, I was on a guide boat that was allowed to come in close to the nesting island, but not close enough for good photographs. Sooty Terns passing overhead gave me just the opportunity I needed.

When you're photographing birds in flight, keep in mind that the exposure can be tricky. White skies will fool most camera meters, requiring up to two stops or more additional exposure than metered. Furthermore, a dark bird against a bright sky will usually need an additional 1/3 to 1/2 stop exposure over the meter reading, while a light bird will need a similar decrease of exposure.

Unless you have a stabilizing lens, try to use a shutter speed of at least 1/125 of a second for flight shots. This will require using a fast lens, relatively fast film, or both. An affordable f/4 lens can get good flight pictures with 200 speed film. Today's films in that speed range are very good.

SPECIALIZED FLIGHT PHOTOGRAPHY

Some birds are either too small or too fast to photograph in flight using the preceding techniques. Birds such as songbirds are perhaps best photographed in flight by letting them photograph themselves.

The birds trip an invisible infrared beam as they fly through it. This requires setting up your equipment along a known line of flight, such as a bird's approach to a nest. Keep in mind that some delay will occur between the breaking of the beam and the release of the shutter. It usually takes a little experimentation to get everything set up just right.

This kind of photography is best practiced in shade, because the flash will be stronger than the ambient light, thereby helping to freeze the motion of the flying bird.

Moderately slow fliers like the Great Egret are much easier to shoot than smaller, faster birds. The contrasting background of open water also helps make this photo effective.

TIP

A photographer is a hunter, but one who doesn't kill anything. With your camera, lead your bird in flight the way a duck hunter leads his quarry.

LIGHT IN FLIGHT

While traveling, I always imagine sunny, blue skies greeting me at my destination. But when I get there, the weather always tells its own story. It might be overcast, or even stormy. So I have learned to be flexible and to try to make the most of any lighting situation when taking photographs of birds.

Early morning and late afternoon light provide pleasing lighting for bird photographs. But pictures taken in different light—sunrises, sunsets, or

Based on information from a friend, the photographer drove three hours to see this Great Gray Owl. A light snow was falling intermittently when he found the bird. The soft, diffused light provided by the overcast sky worked well with the contrast in the stripes and spots of the owl's feather detail.

Glaucous-winged Gulls make their way through thick fog in this moody shot (above). Don't rely on your in-camera meter to render tricky lighting situations like this one. Stormy weather and dramatic light provide an excellent backdrop for a male Common Merganser (below).

stormy weather—can be more interesting. A photograph of a bird hunkered down in a gentle snowfall evokes winter's cold; a flock of birds emerging from a fog bank conveys a sense of mystery. Even when a bird is relatively small in a picture filled with the dramatic light of sunrise or sunset, the image can be stunning.

Tricky lighting situations demand careful attention. In photographs with snow and fog, for instance, your best bet is to set exposure based on a close-up reading or a mid-tone rather than the whole scene. This will likely mean increasing the exposure by a stop or two in order to prevent an underexposed image.

—RULON E. SIMMONS

Don't put the camera away when daylight wanes. Two very different messages and moods were possible with the lone Willet on the beach (opposite) and the Canada Geese crossing a colorful sky (above). Neither image would have worked as well in mid-afternoon.

Following pages:
A dramatic sky was underexposed to produce a mood of tension animated by flying terns.

CHAPTER SIX

CHALLENGES

PHOTOGRAPHING ON THE EDGE

Exciting year-round possibilities await the observant and inquiring bird photographer. Changing seasons, cold weather, and even night-time each provide interesting opportunities.

Before you get out the camera, take some time to study bird behavior. Become familiar with the day-to-day lives and travels of birds. Learn when and where to expect certain birds. Find out the conditions in which birds are more approachable. As you do, you'll figure out new ways to find and photograph them, putting you on the edge where you'll get pictures when others have put their cameras away. Here are a few suggestions.

MIGRATION

Still only partially understood, bird migration is one of the wonders of nature. Long-established patterns of migration, different for each species, are faithfully followed year after year. Consider the astonishing feat of Arctic Terns, which migrate up to 22,000 miles round-trip each year! Then there are the tiny hummingbirds, which make a marathon 500-mile nonstop crossing of the Gulf of Mexico twice a year.

Take advantage of the transitory nature of birds. With a little homework, you can find out where various species are likely to be at any particular time. Many birds winter in southern parts of the United States, including Florida, Texas, and California, where the winters are mild.

Fall plumage on the Palm Warbler and fall foliage on the myrtle bush make an unmistakeable seasonal statement. Migration offers countless opportunities like this.

One problem in photographing these Snow Geese was cleanly separating them by composition from their much larger flock. Showing typical goose behavior, this group consists of feeders and alert guards.

During spring and fall migrations, trips to many of the nation's parks and wildlife refuges along the migratory routes can be very rewarding. Refuge managers and biologists will usually be happy to share their knowledge of local birds and provide you with a bird list for their area. You may not have to go far, either, as city parks are also good places to look for migrating birds.

Fall migration brings many shorebirds to the edges of Lake Ontario, giving me an opportunity to take photographs of species I wouldn't otherwise have a chance to see. Mudflats, with a variety of edible crustaceans and aquatic insects, are also popular stopping areas for migratory shorebirds. Since mud is often difficult to negotiate on foot, make sure you have the right footwear for slogging across the flats.

The fall migration of most shorebirds starts in late July. In my hometown of Rochester, New York, migrating birds are seen in abundance in August and September. These birds are usually in nonbreeding or juvenile plumages. A little earlier in the year, starting around the end of June in the northern states, smaller numbers of shorebirds in breeding plumage can often be found. These are birds that failed to mate and therefore started their southward migration earlier than the rest of the birds.

Considerably fewer shorebirds are seen during the spring migration than in the fall. This is due in part to the high mortality rates they suffer during fall and winter. Also, in the spring, the returning birds are in a hurry to get to their nesting grounds. For both reasons, you are not likely to have as much opportunity to photograph shorebirds in the spring as in the fall.

There are exceptions, though. When horseshoe crabs lay their eggs in May along Delaware Bay, huge numbers of shorebirds come to feast on the eggs. Wherever you do find them, spring birds are often decked out in their striking breeding plumages. During migrations, the birds tend to be less secretive than during the nesting season. This makes photography much easier.

Many excellent places for migrating shorebirds are found along the Atlantic Coast, Cape Cod and Long Island being particularly notable. At certain places along the migratory routes, birds must make long nonstop flights over large bodies of water. After traveling these long distances, some birds, particularly passerines such as warblers and vireos, are tired and will land to rest. When this occurs, a careful photographer can approach birds that would otherwise be very wary. Try not to scare an exhausted bird by coming too close too fast.

NIGHT PHOTOGRAPHY

The following technique is advised primarily for photography of nocturnal birds. It is based on an experience I had as a kid with my ornithologist father. On one particular occasion, I went out on a grouse-banding expedition. We used a generator-powered light to search for birds. That night, I learned that a bird that might otherwise fly off during the day may be approachable at night

TIP

Captive situations offer great opportunities to photograph wildlife. Go to a rehabilitation or nature center to find wounded birds that can't be released. Don't pass up opportunities to shoot these just because they're not in the wild. Even these can make some striking portraits.

when you are essentially hidden behind a veil of light.

If you use this technique, do so only on a limited basis. Diurnal birds cannot make up their sleep. During extreme weather or during the demanding breeding season, disturbance caused by photography can have serious consequences. This technique is much less disturbing to nocturnal birds. Whip-poor-wills and other nightjars are nocturnal birds. Where common, these birds can be located at night by watching for their shining eyes. Once you have located them, you can often approach them quite closely using a spotlight. I have used this approach successfully with Common Pauraques at Bentsen State Park.

I have used night photography on only two occasions to photograph diurnal birds. The first time was to photograph Barn Swallows that I had found nesting under a bridge that crossed a stream. During the daytime, any attempt to get near the birds was met with a rush of wings as the birds scattered from their nests. The situation was dramatically different after dark, when many of the birds could be approached to within inches as they sat on their nests or bridge supports. It was, nevertheless, necessary to move slowly so as not to frighten them.

The challenge of getting good pictures of the Barn Swallows was just beginning, however, once I discovered that I could indeed get close to them. I needed to work out suitable lighting for the pictures and a more stable platform from which to work than my canoe provided. For lighting, I used an electronic flash on each side of my camera.

I needed the second flash to prevent dark shadows on the structure behind the birds. For this flash, I used my underwater unit, which has a built-in slave. To create a more stable platform, I strapped two canoes together with a plank across the top upon which to stand. This gave me good stability and got me up high enough to see more than just heads peering over the nests. It also helped me limit the amount of galvanized steel showing in the picture's background.

I looked for a nest in front of a rusty section for a more natural look. From the pictures, you would never guess that they were taken at night. I used the same technique to photograph an Eastern

The photographer followed these Snow Geese in an airplane long enough to capture the drama of their fall migration.

A Cedar Waxwing (above) spent New Year's Eve sleeping outside the photographer's living room window. The extremely high-speed flash that made the picture possible didn't disturb the bird. The eyes of nocturnal Common Pauraques (below) and other nightjars glow in a beam of light, giving away their presence.

Phoebe that I found nesting under another bridge. Fortunately, this phoebe's nest was low enough to photograph easily from a single canoe. My brief intrusion did not seem to unduly disturb this bird, as it returned to the same nest for several years.

COLD-WEATHER PHOTOGRAPHY

Birds that are very active and difficult to approach under normal conditions may be more approachable during severe winter weather. This includes songbirds that stay year-round in northern climes. Northern Cardinals, for instance, fluff up feathers over their legs and feet to keep warm. In this condition, they are less likely to take flight when they are cautiously approached.

Sometimes in the middle of a harsh winter you can find a stream or other body of open water that will attract a considerable number of birds. Waterbirds such as ducks are consistently found in such places. Excellent opportunities for photography abound when limited open water forces birds to congregate in small areas.

Cold weather also enhances the attractiveness of your bird feeders and birdbaths. Heated birdbaths provide hard-to-find shallow water suitable for drinking and bathing. In winter, when other food is scarce, my children and I have fed Black-capped Chickadees right from our hands!

TIP
Lash a small flashlight under your camera or on top of the flash to help you focus at night.

■ Care of Your Equipment

Winter conditions demand a little extra attention to the care of your equipment. For reliable operation, be sure to keep your camera reasonably warm. The batteries will work more efficiently, and there will be less likelihood of mechanical problems. In extreme cold, film can become brittle. In most situations, simply carrying your camera and some film inside your coat will go a long way to avoiding problems. Take your camera out when you need it, and tuck it back in between shots.

These Chestnut-sided Warblers were photographed during spring migration (above) and fall migration (opposite). High-speed flash stopped the action in both images. A bird's year offers endless opportunities for great photographs.

An external battery pack is another option for many cameras. The pack goes in an inside pocket close to your body to keep the batteries warm. A power cable that runs to the camera can be threaded through a buttonhole.

Protect against condensation, too. When your camera has been in the cold for a while and you bring it inside to warmer, more humid conditions, condensation can form on the lens. To prevent problems, seal your camera in a plastic bag before taking it into a heated area. Let the camera warm up, then remove the bag.

For necessary dexterity to operate the shutter release in cold weather, I use a glove without fingertips. In extremely cold weather, a thin silk or cotton glove worn under the glove with missing fingertips offers extra warmth.

HOT-WEATHER PHOTOGRAPHY

When the weather is hot, your best opportunities for bird photography will often be early in the morning or later in the evening, when relatively cool temperatures prevail. If you have to be out during the hottest time of day, be sure to take care of yourself. Drink plenty of fluids, wear a hat with a brim, and wear sunscreen. Take mosquito repellent. You'll probably need it in the watery environments where you'll be most likely to find birds.

YEAR-ROUND PHOTOGRAPHY

Time of year plays an important part in determining the subjects you will find. Whether you choose to travel or stay at home, you can find abundant opportunities for bird photography throughout the year. Here's a year-round scenario for bird photography that will apply to many areas of the United States.

■ Spring

Spring, a season with all sorts of photographic possibilities, is characterized by dramatic breeding plumages, singing birds, and an increased variety of birds showing up at feeders as spring migration gets under way. Remember to check nearby lakes and ponds for spring migrants.

Start watching for nesting birds in the spring and continue looking for them into the summer.

TIP

Drip pools are especially effective in attracting birds during migration, when the birds have been flying long distances and are in search of water and respite.

During the nesting season, you could try luring some common birds with bird song recordings. Check the regulations in the areas where you want to take pictures before you go.

In some places, luring birds with recordings is illegal because it can chase birds from their habitats. Overeager birders, playing recordings in order to see a bird, can have a detrimental effect. Avoid being part of the problem by minimizing the use of recordings to lure birds.

■ **Summer**

During the summer, birds such as Mourning Doves, House Finches, American Goldfinches, various sparrows, and grackles continue to come to feeders. Don't expect to see as many different kinds of birds as in winter or during migrations, however. On summer trips, plan stops for photography at national parks and wildlife refuges.

Toward the end of summer, most birds molt, gradually losing their old feathers and getting new ones. The birds can look pretty ragged at this time of year, but they can still make very interesting subjects for photographs. Birds can be harder to find because they aren't singing. Since nesting activities have been completed, birds aren't singing for territorial defense and courtship. Some species must be careful during this time because they are more vulnerable to predators as their feathers molt.

Your best opportunities for bird photography at the end of summer may well be with migrating shorebirds found on mudflats, lakeshores, or in freshly plowed fields.

◼ Fall

In the fall, excitement builds at feeders again as the southward migration brings new birds to your neighborhood. Put out some suet when the hot days of summer have waned, and you will likely see a variety of birds. The list of visitors could include woodpeckers, chickadees, nuthatches, and others, depending upon where you live. Continue checking beaches, mudflats, and plowed fields for migrating shorebirds.

Reflected fall colors make a beautiful setting for this photograph of a lone American Wigeon.

Following pages: Fresh snow simplifies an otherwise complex background, allowing a male Northern Cardinal to stand out as the center of interest no matter how small he appears in the photograph.

■ Winter

Don't put your camera away during the winter. There will continue to be a lot of activity at your feeders. The scarcity of food will bring new varieties of birds not seen at other times.

In the northern United States, winter species include birds such as juncos, nuthatches, chickadees, woodpeckers, and occasionally redpolls or other northern finches. A variety of different sparrows (e.g., Fox, Swamp, Song, White-throated, Vesper, Le Conte's, Savannah, and Grasshopper) choose to live in southern states during the winter. American Goldfinches, Purple Finches, and Red-breasted Nuthatches also frequent winter feeders in the South. On the West Coast, look for Golden- and White-crowned Sparrows.

During the winter, also check beaches for gull species that may not reside year-round in your locality. Note that gulls that have black heads in the summer will lose the dark plumage on their heads during the winter, providing an opportunity for comparison shots. Look for Heermann's, Mew, Western, California, and Glaucous-winged gulls on western winter beaches. Keep in mind that in some species only the younger birds migrate as far south as California. In the East, expect to find Bonaparte's, Great Black-backed, and Laughing gulls. Ring-billed and Herring gulls are common along the eastern and western coasts of the United States.

As seasons change, as temperatures plummet, and as day turns to night, look for ever changing opportunities for bird photography. You should be able to photograph a wide variety of birds throughout the year.

No winner of a beauty contest during molting, this nearly bald, apologetic-looking Blue Jay (above) nevertheless tells of the changing seasons. Note the insect-eaten leaves of August.

This female Red-breasted Merganser (opposite) is similar to an immature male. The male has redder eyes and bill and more white on the wing.

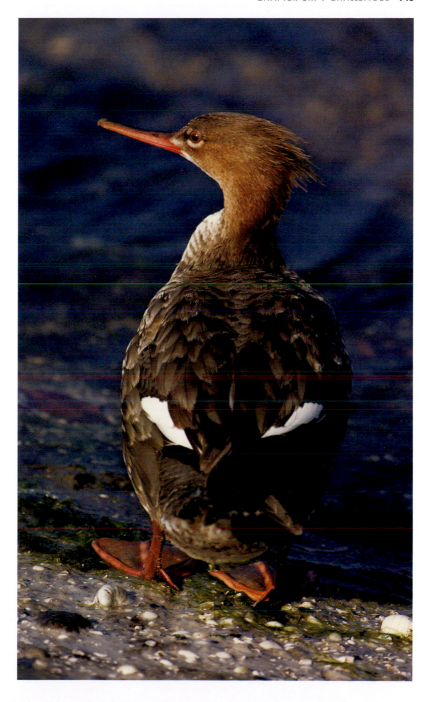

ETHICS IN DIGITAL

Because Adobe Photoshop is such a powerful tool for manipulating a photograph, the question of ethics arises. You must make some decisions about the number and kind of alterations you want to apply to your own work. It's easy when you work for a client who lays down the rules for acceptance, refusing to publish any even slightly retouched photograph. Your own personal statements are a different matter.

I once saw a photograph of a woman turning into an owl. Her body was human, but her face was barred owl. It was beautifully "Photoshopped."

This photograph of a Northern Cardinal can easily be manipulated using such powerful programs as Photoshop. In the opposite image, the background leaves and branches have been blurred out to accentuate the central image. Such changes render the photograph artificial and should always be disclosed in the caption.

The composite illustration on the opposite page creates a photograph that never actually existed. This level of manipulation creates a new and false product that most editors would consider unethical.

I loved it. Of course, it was not meant to fool the viewer but rather to cause a reaction. It succeeded in its purpose.

On another occasion, I saw a photograph of a bird in a background that was well suited to the mood and composition. The photographer later admitted the bird had been shot against another background and removed to the new one. "That original background was cluttered and just didn't work with the bird," confided the photographer. Ethical or not? It fooled me, but it was only shown to friends and not the public. Ultimately, you must be the judge. Before the days of digital printing, some bird photographers would sandwich two transparencies together, then make a copy for slide projection. I did a beauty of geese flying across a setting sun. I explained how I made it when I gave my slide show, but I'm sure some purists in the audience were offended. With Photoshop, this can be done with much greater ease and speed. The temptation lurks out there in the shadowy world of ethics.

"I use Photoshop to clone out obtrusive branches or out-of-focus weeds in my bird photography," says one shooter (who would never tell his audience or publisher). "I manipulated this shot," says another. "I started with that cloudy mountain scenic and then put the flying raven in right there as the center of interest. It's an illustration, not journalism. I like the picture a lot."

Are there manipulated photographs in this book? Would you care if there were? Would you even know if you were not told? I can't see, though, how cheating would make this particular book any better. Cheating!? It surely is that if the trickery is not divulged. But what if one uses trickery to tell lies and then labels it art or an illustration and puts in in a book? Is that cheating? Is that ethical?

Advertisers manipulate photographs all the time. Ad art directors are the poster boys for digital liars. Does that make the business unethical? Do people look at ads and say, "I won't buy that product because the picture has obviously been manipulated"?

Whatever you decide to use as your own guidelines, remember that these serious questions have been asked since the beginning of photography.

—BATES LITTLEHALES

WHERE TO SHOOT

FAVORITE LOCATIONS

Not all good birding areas are equally good locations for photography. One of the best ways to get close-up pictures of birds is to go to areas where birds are plentiful and used to seeing "friendly" people. Such areas include national, state, and local parks, national wildlife refuges, private sanctuaries, and public beaches.

Make your trip more rewarding by obtaining local birding guide books. Note that some species listed for the following locations can only be found at certain times during the year. Check with field guides and local birders for current conditions and best times to see different species. There are many excellent places for bird photography in the United States and Canada. Some of my favorites are described below.

ALASKA

■ Kenai Peninsula

Kenai Peninsula has a variety of forest birds. In Homer, you can find Northwestern Crows, Glaucous-winged Gulls, Bald Eagles, and various waterfowl, including Trumpeter Swans.

■ Pribilof Islands

A flight to Saint Paul will get you to one of the best places in Alaska to photograph seabird colonies. Tour buses are the only means of transportation. The best seabird cliffs are on the southern edge of the island, at Ridge Wall and Southwest Point. You can photograph Common

A Little Blue Heron resting in mangroves perfectly conveys the idea of a bird at home in its habitat. The photographer made this picture through a car window along a wildlife drive in Florida's Darling National Wildlife Refuge.

and Thick-billed murres, Black-legged and Red-legged kittiwakes, auklets, Horned and Tufted puffins, Northern Fulmars, Red-faced Cormorants, Gray-crowned Rosy Finches, even Northern Fur Seals.

ARIZONA
More than 300 species of birds are found in south-eastern Arizona, some of which occur nowhere else in the United States.

■ The Arizona-Sonora Desert Museum
On a one-day visit, I photographed Curve-billed Thrashers, Gila Woodpeckers, Gilded Flickers, Pyrrhuloxias, Phainopeplas, and Cactus Wrens.

Northern Gannets of Bonaventure Island, Canada, clap their bills together in a courtship display. Be prepared, then wait for the moment that can make a picture special. Patience pays off.

You can also photograph native birds in an aviary.

■ Cave Creek Canyon

Scenic Cave Creek Canyon is near the town of Portal. Acorn Woodpeckers abound; you may also find Arizona Woodpeckers. Many other birds are found in this desert oasis. Several species of hummingbird frequent feeders in Portal and at the Southwestern Research Station. Also check for birds at Stewart Campground, Rustler Park, and Cave Creek Ranch. Listen for the sounds of Elegant Trogons at South Fork and along Barefoot Peak Trail, leading from the campground into the canyon. At dusk, look and listen for Whiskered Screech-Owls and Whip-poor-wills. In summer, a hummingbird feeder set up at any of the campgrounds in the canyon should attract many species, including the Blue-throated Hummingbird.

■ Madera Canyon

Madera Canyon is located between Tucson and Nogales. Birders come here to look for the rare Elegant Trogon as well as a variety of canyon woodland species.

In summer, look for Black-chinned, Broad-billed, Blue-throated, and Magnificent hummingbirds. Try setting up a feeder at Bog Springs Campground. Opportunities in winter are spectacular. You should be able to find Mexican Jays, Bridled Titmice, Yellow-eyed Juncos, Dark-eyed Juncos (Oregon and Gray-headed subspecies), Acorn Woodpeckers, and White-breasted Nuthatches at seed feeders at the Madera Lodge.

In grasslands below Madera Canyon, you can look for Cassin's Sparrow, Botteri's Sparrow, Rufous-winged Sparrow, and Varied Bunting. In rocky washes nearby, you may find the Buff-collared Nightjar (a rare Mexican species). Watch where you go and beware of rattlesnakes—I almost stepped on one!

■ Ramsey Canyon

Mile-Hi Ranch in Ramsey Canyon, run by the Nature Conservancy, has been described as the hummingbird capital of the United States. Twelve species of hummingbird are known to visit this ranch. There's a bank of feeders near the Visitors Center, but they are not well positioned for photography. In the valley below Ramsey Canyon, I found and photographed Scaled Quail, Greater Roadrunners, and Curve-billed Thrashers.

CALIFORNIA

■ Los Angeles Area

About a mile northwest of the Los Angeles International Airport, Del Rey Lagoon is an exceptionally good place to find and photograph birds in winter. I have photographed Lesser

Scaup, Buffleheads, American Wigeons, Red-breasted Mergansers, Pacific Loons, Long-billed Dowitchers, Willets, Spotted Sandpipers, American Coots, Brewer's Blackbirds, gulls, and hummingbirds there. A block north of Del Rey Lagoon, along a channel leading from Playa del Rey, look for gulls, terns, grebes (Western, Horned, and Eared), Surf Scoters, Pelagic Cormorants, and various shorebirds such as Willets, Marbled Godwits, Whimbrels, Surfbirds, Black Oystercatchers, and turnstones (Ruddy and Black).

At Bolsa Chica Ecological Reserve, near Huntington Beach in Orange County, look for a variety of ducks, shorebirds, and terns. Expect to see Surf Scoters, Blue-winged Teal, Buffleheads, Northern Pintails, Ruddy Ducks, Lesser Scaup,

Western and Eared Grebes, several kinds of sparrows, and a variety of shorebirds.

South along the Pacific Coast Highway, along Upper Newport Bay, I photographed three species of teal as well as American Avocets in mid-January. (I returned a month later and again found all teal species present.) Also within camera range were American Wigeons and a variety of shorebirds, including a Long-billed Curlew. The uncommon Clapper Rail is a resident here. High tide is the best time to visit, as the higher water forces the birds closer to the road.

■ Monterey Bay
Monterey Bay is an excellent place to find pelagic birds. In the harbor area, you should be able to

A Great Egret stalks the salt marshes of Delaware Bay. This much photographed bird works beautifully as a center of interest in landscapes because of its contrasting white plumage.

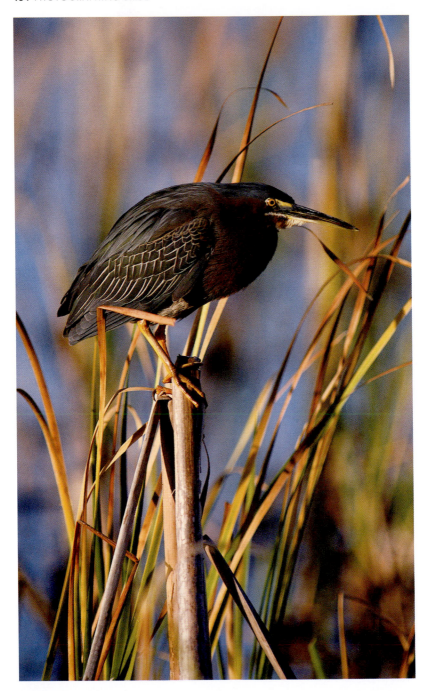

photograph Brandt's and Pelagic Cormorants and Pigeon Guillemots. Pelagic boat trips that depart from this location can bring you close to shearwaters, jaegers, storm-petrels, and more.

At Pt. Lobos Reserve State Park, located along the south shore of Carmel Bay, not far from Monterey Bay, and at Point Pinos in Pacific Grove, you will have a chance to photograph various birds, including Black Oystercatchers, Black Turnstones, and Surfbirds.

■ Salton Sea National Wildlife Refuge

A good area for photography is along Garst Road, leading to the Red Hill Marina. In season, look for nesting Great Blue Herons. At the Salton Sea, I've photographed Herring Gulls, Yellow-footed Gulls, Black-necked Stilts, American Coots, Eared Grebes, Ruddy Ducks, Northern Shovelers, and Burrowing Owls, all from my car window.

Burrowing Owls are found along the dikes and ditches of Sinclair Road, which leads to the refuge headquarters. Yellow-footed Gulls are fairly common in the summer; these birds are very rarely seen at any other location in the United States.

■ San Diego Area

Check San Diego Bay, particularly Strand Beach, for shorebirds. I got some nice Long-billed Curlew shots there. Ask about the biological study area at the southwestern end.

About two miles south of Silver Strand, Tijuana Slough National Wildlife Refuge is a good place to find and photograph shorebirds, waterfowl, gulls, terns, and Savannah Sparrows. I also made some great pictures of a Say's Phoebe there one day.

The Mission Bay area is also a good place to find approachable shorebirds. Look for Willets, Whimbrels, and Yellowlegs. Gulls are also plentiful. A little further north is the La Jolla Cove,

A Green Heron perches by a pond in Everglades National Park. In many parks and refuges, birds are used to people and will allow photographers to approach quite closely if they do so in a calm and quiet way.

which attracts marine mammals and birds in great numbers.

■ Tule Lake and Lower Klamath National Wildlife Refuges

Tule Lake National Wildlife Refuge and the nearby Lower Klamath National Wildlife Refuge, near the California-Oregon border, are excellent places to find waterfowl, including Greater White-fronted Geese, Snow Geese, Ross's Geese, Northern Pintails, Mallards, Northern Shovelers, Cinnamon Teal, Green-winged Teal, Canvasbacks, Redheads, American Wigeons, Gadwall, Ruddy Ducks, American Coots, and several species of grebes.

Ring-necked Pheasants and California Quail are also plentiful along the roads. You will see eagles here November through March, but probably won't get close enough for good pictures. There are photo blinds and a wildlife drive. October to November is the best time to visit. At Klamath Falls, where the river drains the Klamath Lake, you can get very close to Barrow's and Common Goldeneyes.

■ Yosemite

Yosemite National Park offers spectacular scenery as well as great birding. I photographed Steller's Jays at a roadside turnoff overlooking the valley. Look for Blue Grouse in isolated pine stands south of Olmsted Point. They are usually easy to approach and photograph. The Bridal Veil Campground area on the road to Glacier Point is one of the best areas for a variety of montane wood-land bird species.

COLORADO

■ Rocky Mountain National Park

For montane birds, visit Rocky Mountain National Park, where you can find Steller's Jays, Mountain Chickadees, Broad-tailed Hummingbirds (and other hummingbirds during migration), Clark's Nutcrackers, Gray Jays, Western Wood-Pewees, American Dippers, and wood-peckers. White-tailed Ptarmigan, found above timberline along Trail Ridge Road, are difficult

Early morning light silhouettes a flock of roosting Sandhill Cranes as they leave for a day of foraging. Scout an area for birds, learn their comings and goings, and be ready to take advantage of photo opportunities like this one.

to find but tame. Park rangers can tell you where to look for ptarmigan.

FLORIDA

■ Dry Tortugas and Florida Keys

The Dry Tortugas, a group of tiny islets located 70 miles west of Key West, have drawn birders for years. Bush Key, Loggerhead Key , and Garden Key are the principal islets and can be reached only by boat or seaplane.

I recommend going by chartered boat. Access to the nesting grounds for Sooty Terns, Brown Noddies, Magnificent Frigatebirds, and a few Masked Boobies is restricted. Boats are allowed in the surrounding water, though generally not close enough for close-up photos.

Your best chance of getting pictures of Sooty Terns is to photograph them as they fly to their nests. The easiest place to photograph Brown Noddies is at Garden Key, where they often line up on the rusting remains of an old pier. Frigatebirds ride thermals above Fort Jefferson. You can get close to them from the roof of the fort, which is accessible to the general public.

In late April and early May, look for migrating songbirds on Garden Key, particularly inside the fort. During or just after a storm, you may see dozens of different warblers, thrushes, and other songbirds weak from their long flight over water. During such a "fallout," exhausted birds can be approached easily, and photographed. Water drips set up in the campground and inside the fort often provide for excellent photographic opportunities.

Boat trips leave from the vicinity of Key West. In a well-timed spring drive down the Keys, you may find White-crowned Pigeons, Gray Kingbirds, American Redstarts, Blackpoll Warblers, and Northern Parulas—I did! Take some time to explore this wide area for the right location.

Black-necked Stilts are one of the common shorebirds found at Salton Sea National Wildlife Refuge. This photo was taken along the refuge road, from a car. Keep in mind the direction and quality of light as you compose your pictures.

■ Everglades National Park

Everglades National Park offers a great diversity of bird life. Many birds are so used to people that they can be approached closely: Snowy, Great, and Cattle egrets, Great Blue Herons, Green Herons, Anhingas, Least Bitterns, American Bitterns, American Coots, Common Moorhens, Purple Gallinules, Turkey Vultures, Black Vultures, American Crows, Red-shouldered Hawks, Roseate Spoonbills, Pied-billed Grebes, Brown Pelicans, Black-necked Stilts, White Ibises, Wood Storks, and Black-crowned Night-Herons.

The Scissor-tailed Flycatcher arrives in Texas in early spring. The bird sits in one place before darting after prey, making it fairly easy to photograph.

Look for Brown Pelicans near the fishing docks at Flamingo. "Head and shoulders" portraits are possible with a 100mm lens. Anhinga Trail includes a boardwalk into a marshy area where birds can be found at all times of the year. Frequently seen birds along this trail include Great Blue, Green, and Little Blue herons, American and Least bitterns, American Coots, Common Moorhens, Purple Gallinules, Pied-billed Grebes, and of course Anhingas. In spring, you have a good chance of finding birds nesting close to the trail.

■ Sanibel Island

A wide variety of waterbirds such as Anhingas, Yellow-crowned Night-Herons, Brown Pelicans, Wood Storks, Roseate Spoonbills, as well as various herons and ducks can be obseved at close range at J. N. "Ding" Darling National Wildlife Refuge. Turkey Vultures, Fish Crows, and Brown Pelicans are also common. Several Osprey nests are located in the refuge and at nearby locations. You can photograph from your car along a five-mile drive.

■ Wakodahatchee

North of Miami, on the west side of Delray Beach, Wakodahatchee is a new wetland and water-treatment facility, completed in 1996. In just a few years, it has attracted egrets, herons, anhingas, and many other kinds of water and land birds. More than 140 bird species have been recorded at the site.

A boardwalk at the facility puts visitors close to the birds, making it an excellent location for photography. Least Bitterns (in season) and Purple Gallinules, uncommon birds in most Florida locations, can be found here easily. Also look for Limpkins, Green Herons, Least Terns, Mottled Ducks, American Coots, Common Moorhens, Red-winged Blackbirds, Tricolored Herons, and several species of egret.

MAINE
■ Machias Seal Island
Machias Seal Island, located between Maine (U.S.) and New Brunswick (Canada) is a nesting site for Atlantic Puffins. There are photo blinds on the island, from which it is easy to photograph Razorbills, Atlantic Puffins, and Arctic Terns. Charter boats are available for travel to the island.

NEW JERSEY
■ Cape May
Fall migration at Cape May can only be described as spectacular. Birds accumulate there during their southward migration, as they make their way to shore or prepare to make the 16-mile journey over the Delaware Bay. Passerines of all sorts can be found. The profusion of Northern Flickers makes for a remarkable sight. September is the best month to visit.

In spring, you can also find a variety of shorebirds, herons, gulls, and terns at Reed's Beach and Stone Harbor Point. At South Cape May Meadow, you will find shorebirds and herons. Piping Plovers and Least Terns nest there and can be photographed.

At Stone Harbor, located north of Cape May, herons can be photographed on their nests from a reasonable range. Snowy Egrets, Cattle Egrets, Great Egrets, Glossy Ibises, Black-crowned and Yellow-crowned Night Herons, Great Blue Herons, Tricolored Herons, and an occasional Little Blue Heron also roost there.

■ Edwin B. Forsythe National Wildlife Refuge

During migrations, the Edwin B. Forsythe (Brigantine) National Wildlife Refuge is an excellent refuge for shorebirds, including dowitchers, Whimbrels, Dunlins, and Black-bellied Plovers. Look for Clapper Rails along the canals. May and August to September are good times to visit. In late autumn, thousands of Snow Geese as well as Canada Geese can be found at the refuge. There are auto routes and photo blinds.

NEW MEXICO
■ Bosque Del Apache National Wildlife Refuge

Bosque del Apache National Wildlife Refuge is the wintering ground for large numbers of Sandhill Cranes and Snow Geese. Ducks are also plentiful. The best time to photograph is from late November through early February. The first time I visited the refuge, in mid-November, there were approximately 6,000 Sandhill Cranes and 25,000 to 30,000 Snow Geese.

On my first trip, I was able to get pictures showing geese covering the ground like a carpet of snow. In winter, they come right up to the roads to feed on grain. I photographed Snow Geese at close range from my car and even got some shots of a lone Ross's Goose.

In spring, look for Western Kingbirds nesting near the Visitors Center, Ash-throated Flycatchers on low bushes, and Ring-necked Pheasants along the auto loop. Gambel's Quail are fed year-round on the east side of the Visitor's Center.

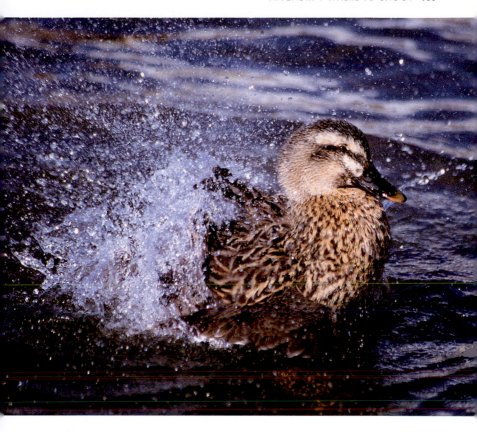

A small dome tent, which I set up about ten feet from the feeding area, worked very well as a blind.

NEW YORK

■ New York City Area

Nearly every kind of shorebird found in the eastern United States migrates through Jamaica Bay. Late July through early September is the best time for a visit. Brant are plentiful in winter. On Long Island's southern shore, there are several good areas, including Jones Beach (where Common and Roseate Terns nest), Fire Island, Moriches Inlet, and Montauk Point. June and July are the best times to visit. Check Central Park for migrating passerines.

Mallards are common in many city parks and ponds, such as Del Rey Lagoon in Los Angeles. Note that in the midst of all the frenzied splashing in this image, the bird's eye remains in focus.

NORTH DAKOTA
■ J. Clark Salyer National Wildlife Refuge

At J. Clark Salyer National Wildlife Refuge, you can photograph Franklin's Gulls (which nest there), Yellow-headed Blackbirds, American White Pelicans, and many kinds of waterfowl.

Look in grassland areas for Baird's Sparrow, Sprague's Pipits, LeConte's Sparrows, and Sharp-tailed Sparrows. Try the refuge blind in May for photographs of Sharp-tailed Grouse.

RHODE ISLAND
■ Sachuest Point National Wildlife Refuge

Sachuest Point National Wildlife Refuge is noted for Harlequin Ducks, which reside here from November through April. Harlequin Ducks frequent rocky coastlines. With care they can be approached for photographs. The birds often swim very close to shore, but somehow they always seem to stay just out of good camera range when they are in the water.

I have had my best luck approaching birds that were resting on the rocks. Other birds to look for at Sachuest Point are Common Eiders, Common Goldeneyes, Buffleheads, Horned and Red-necked grebes, Red-breasted Mergansers, Common and Red-throated loons, and the three species of scoter.

SOUTH DAKOTA
■ Sand Lake National Wildlife Refuge

In March and early April, countless Snow Geese make a stop at Sand Lake National Wildlife Refuge, located northeast of Aberdeen and home to more than 266 species of birds. In August and September, this same refuge hosts several hundred thousand Franklin's Gulls, which stop there during their southward migration. American White Pelicans and various wading birds are also found at the refuge.

TEXAS

■ Aransas National Wildlife Refuge

Aransas is best known for the rare Whooping Cranes that winter there. To see the cranes, private groups run boat trips that last about four hours. The refuge Visitors Center has information on the trips. If you take a morning boat trip, you will usually have the best sun position for photography. In addition to Whooping Cranes, you may be able to photograph Roseate Spoonbills, many herons, Black Vultures, Turkey Vultures, and Caspian Terns.

■ Bentsen State Park

Feeders here attract South Texas specialties such as the Altamira Oriole. The park is unsurpassed for photographing the Common Pauraque. Look for the birds at night along roads and grassy margins. They are easy to see because their eyes reflect car headlights.

This Semipalmated Sandpiper, tending her brood by the side of the road just outside Nome, Alaska, allowed close approach as the photographer moved slowly toward the bird with a 70-210mm zoom lens.

■ Padre Island National Seashore

Padre Island is a long, skinny barrier island extending from Corpus Christi, Texas, to the southern tip of the state. Road access is limited. Here, at Padre Island National Seashore, I was able to photograph Royal, Sandwich, and Least Terns and an American Oystercatcher, using my car as a blind. Birding all along the Texas coast is good year-round, but the spring shorebird migration is particularly notable.

■ Santa Ana National Wildlife Refuge

Santa Ana National Wildlife Refuge is noted for subtropical birds found in few other locations north of Mexico. The Plain Chachalaca, a chickenlike bird, is found here in abundance. Waterfowl and shorebirds are also plentiful. Other birds to look for include Least and Pied-billed

Concealed behind a blind, the photographer shot this handsome close-up portrait of a Tufted Puffin with a 600mm lens.

grebes, Green Kingfishers (rare), American Coots, Common Moorhens, and Great Kiskadees. I have photographed Plain Chachalacas, Green Jays, White-tipped Doves, Altamira Orioles, and Black-crested Titmice at Santa Ana. A feeding station near the Visitors Center attracts many of these species.

VIRGINIA
■ Chincoteague National Wildlife Refuge
The refuge hosts Snow and Canada Geese, Laughing Gulls, Mute Swans, Yellow-crowned Night-Herons, Green Herons, Clapper Rails, shorebirds, and others.

WYOMING
■ Yellowstone National Park
Yellowstone provides many opportunities to take

pictures of Trumpeter Swans, Common Ravens, and Clark's Nutcrackers. Trumpeter Swans, now making a comeback from the brink of extinction, are often seen along the Madison River. In Yellowstone, you can get close enough to ravens to obtain full-frame photos using a 600mm lens.

Stop at the Bridge Bay Picnic Area for shots of Clark's Nutcrackers and Gray Jays. These birds fly around the picnic tables picking up food scraps.

CANADA

■ Bonaventure Island

This island in Quebec is the site of a large Northern Gannet rookery. It is accessible only by boats, which make the 15-minute trip from Percé several times a day. Visitors must hike for about 45 minutes to get to the nesting area. Birds can easily be photographed on the ground or in flight. Nesting occurs from June through September.

■ Fort Erie

Tens of thousands of gulls congregate along the Niagara River in the vicinity of Niagara Falls during late fall and early winter. Most are Bonaparte's, Ring-billed, Great Black-backed, and Herring Gulls. Black-legged Kittiwakes and Sabine's, Franklin's, and Little Gulls and other rarities are occasionally found. Most observation points along the river are at the top of the gorge, where cameras are of little value. At Fort Erie, on the Canadian side, the road runs along the riverbank. Gulls often feed right near the shore.

■ Point Pelee

Point Pelee, on the northern shore of Lake Erie in Ontario, is a great birding spot during spring and fall migrations. Because it juts out into Lake Erie, it is a natural attraction for migrating birds looking for a place to rest before or after their long flights over the lake.

WAYS TO GET CLOSE TO BIRDS

This table lists recommended methods of getting close to different birds to photograph them. Keep in mind that these recommendations are quite subjective. For example, a particular bird species might be very approachable in one area and less so in others. Photography at nests is dependent on first being able to find a nest that is accessible. In general, if a bird can be attracted with food, that will be the best way to get close to it for photography. If a bird is not too secretive or shy, then stalking may work well. Otherwise, you may have to find a nest or use a recording to get close-up pictures.

Albatross	Nest	Duck (diving)	Stalk
Anhinga	Stalk	Duck (surface feeding)	Food
Ani	Stalk	Dunlin	Stalk
Auklet	Nest	Eagle	Stalk
Avocet	Stalk	Egret	Stalk
Becard	Stalk	Falcon	Stalk
Bittern	Stalk	Finch	Food
Blackbird	Stalk	Flamingo	Stalk
Blackbird, Red-winged	Recording	Flicker	Nest
Bluebird	Nest	Flycatcher	Stalk
Bobolink	Stalk	Frigatebird	Nest
Bobwhite	Food	Fulmar	Nest
Booby	Nest	Gallinule	Stalk
Bulbul	Stalk	Gannet	Nest
Bunting	Stalk	Gnatcatcher	Recording
Bushtit	Stalk	Godwit	Stalk
Caracara	Stalk	Goldfinch	Food
Cardinal	Food	Goose	Stalk
Catbird	Recording	Grackle	Food
Chachalaca	Food	Grebe	Stalk
Chat	Nest	Grosbeak	Food
Chickadee	Food	Grouse	Lek
Chuck-will's-widow	Stalk	Guillemot	Nest
Coot	Stalk	Gull	Food
Cormorant	Stalk	Hawk	Stalk
Cowbird	Food	Heron	Stalk
Crane	Stalk	Hummingbird	Food
Creeper	Stalk	Ibis	Stalk
Crossbill	Food	Jacana	Stalk
Crow	Stalk	Jaeger	Stalk
Cuckoo	Stalk	Jay	Food
Curlew	Stalk	Junco	Food
Dickcissel	Food	Kestrel	Nest box
Dipper	Stalk	Killdeer	Nest
Dove	Food	Kingbird	Stalk
Dowitcher	Stalk	Kingfisher	Stalk

Kinglet	Stalk	Roadrunner	Stalk
Kiskadee	Stalk	Robin	Stalk
Kite	Stalk	Ruff	Stalk
Kittiwake	Nest	Sanderling	Stalk
Knot	Stalk	Sandpiper	Stalk
Lapwing	Stalk	Shearwater	Stalk
Lark	Nest	Shrike	Stalk
Limpkin	Stalk	Siskin	Food
Longspur	Stalk	Skimmer	Stalk
Loon	Stalk	Snipe	Stalk
Magpie	Stalk	Solitaire	Stalk
Martin	Nest	Sparrow	Food
Meadowlark	Stalk	Sparrow, House	Food
Mockingbird	Stalk	Spoonbill	Stalk
Moorhen	Stalk	Starling	Food
Murre	Nest	Stilt	Stalk
Murrelet	Nest	Surfbird	Stalk
Nighthawk	Nest	Swallow	Nest
Nutcracker	Food	Swan	Stalk
Nuthatch	Food	Swift	Nest
Oriole	Nest	Tanager	Nest
Osprey	Nest	Tern	Stalk
Ovenbird	Nest	Thrasher	Stalk
Owl	Recording	Thrush	Stalk
Oystercatcher	Stalk	Titmouse	Food
Partridge	Food	Towhee	Stalk
Pauraque	Stalk	Trogon	Nest
Pelican	Stalk	Tropicbird	Nest
Petrel	Stalk	Turkey	Recording
Pewee	Nest	Turnstone	Stalk
Phalarope	Stalk	Veery	Nest
Pheasant	Food	Verdin	Stalk
Phoebe	Nest	Vireo	Nest
Pigeon	Food	Vulture	Stalk
Pipit	Stalk	Warbler	Nest
Plover	Stalk	Waterthrush	Stalk
Poorwill	Stalk	Waxwing	Stalk
Ptarmigan	Stalk	Whimbrel	Stalk
Puffin	Nest	Whip-poor-will	Stalk
Pyrrhuloxia	Food	Willet	Stalk
Quail	Food	Woodcock	Stalk
Rail	Stalk	Woodpecker	Food
Raven	Stalk	Wren	Nest
Razorbill	Nest	Wrentit	Nest
Redpoll	Food	Yellowlegs	Stalk
Redstart	Nest	Yellowthroat	Stalk

RECOMMENDED FOOD AND FEEDERS

Bird	Food	Feeder
Blackbird	Cracked Grain, Millet	Ground or Hanging
Bluebird, Eastern	Peanut Butter Mix, Dried Fruit	Hanging (winter)
Bunting, Indigo	Millet	Ground or Hanging
Bunting, Lazuli	Millet	Ground or Hanging
Cardinal	Sunflower Seeds	Ground or Hanging
Catbird	Oranges, Raisins	Ground
Chickadee	Sunflower Seeds, Suet	Hanging
Cowbird	Cracked Grain, Millet	Ground or Hanging
Creeper	Suet, Peanut Butter Mix	Spread on Tree Bark
Crossbill	Sunflower Seeds	Hanging
Crow	Cracked Grain	Ground
Dove	Cracked Corn, Millet	Ground
Finch	Sunflower Seeds, Millet	Hanging or Ground
Flicker	Suet, Peanut Butter Mix	Ground (winter)
Goldfinch	Niger Seed	Hanging
Grackle	Cracked Grain	Ground or Hanging
Grosbeak, Black-headed	Sunflower Seeds	Hanging (winter)
Grosbeak, Evening	Sunflower Seeds	Hanging or Ground
Grosbeak, Rose-breasted	Sunflower Seeds	Hanging
Grouse	Cracked Corn, Soybeans	Ground
Hummingbird	Sugar Water	Hanging
Jay	Whole Peanuts, Sunflower Seeds	Hanging or Ground
Junco	Millet	Ground
Mallard	Cracked Corn, Bread	Near/On Shore
Meadowlark	Cracked Grain	Ground
Mockingbird	Raisins, Suet	Ground
Nutcracker, Clark's	Suet, Bread, Peanuts	Ground
Nuthatch	Suet, Sunflower Seeds	Hanging
Oriole	Sugar Water, Oranges	Hanging
Pheasant	Cracked Corn, Soybeans	Ground
Pigeon	Cracked Corn, Millet	Ground
Quail	Cracked Corn, Soybeans	Ground
Redpoll	Niger Seed, Millet	Hanging or Ground
Robin	Sliced Apples, Peanut Butter	Ground
Siskin	Niger Seed, Millet	Hanging or Ground
Sparrow	Millet, Cracked Corn	Ground
Sparrow, House	Millet, Cracked Corn	Ground or Hanging
Starling	Suet, Bread Crumbs	Ground or Hanging
Tanager	Sugar Water, Suet	High Hanging
Thrush, Hermit	Raisins, Suet	Ground, Low Platform
Titmouse	Sunflower Seeds, Suet	Hanging
Towhee	Millet, Cracked Corn	Ground
Turkey	Cracked Corn	Ground
Warbler, Yellow-rumped	Suet, Peanut Butter Mix	Platform (winter)
Woodpecker	Suet, Peanut Butter Mix	Attached to Tree Trunk
Wren, Carolina	Suet, Peanut Hearts	Hanging

EQUIPMENT

Camera Bag Essentials

- camera bag lined with foam-rubber compartments
- camera body with body cap and neck strap
- favorite lenses with lens caps
- lens hoods
- handheld exposure meter
- film of various ISO ratings or digital cards for digital cameras
- air blower brush
- lens cleaner solution and lens tissue wipes
- tripod, monopod, and/or bean bags
- gaffer's tape
- electronic flash
- extra camera, exposure meter, and flash batteries
- remote release
- equipment manuals

Options

- binoculars
- blinds
- spotting scope
- filters such as UV haze, skylight 1A, polarizing, neutral density, graded neutral density, light amber, light blue
- plastic bag or sheet to protect equipment in wet weather
- soft absorbent towel or chamois
- silica gel for wet weather
- large umbrella
- cooler and freezable gel packs for hot weather
- extra camera body
- extra electronic flash
- extra handheld exposure meter

- selenium cell exposure meter that operates in cold weather
- notebook and permanent marker
- self-stick labels to identify film
- sunglasses
- head and wrist sweatbands
- camouflage clothing
- gray card
- resealable plastic bags for storing film
- customized diopter to match your eyeglass prescription
- reflectors
- slave units and radio transmitter for electronic flash
- extension tubes
- teleconverters
- film x-ray bag for air travel

Tool Kit

- film changing bag
- film leader retriever
- Swiss army knife
- filter wrench
- small socket wrenches
- jeweler's screwdrivers
- tweezers
- needle-nosed pliers to loosen jammed tripod joints
- pencil eraser to clean connections

Safety Kit

- flashlight
- compass
- whistle
- water and snacks
- first aid kit
- reflective tape (for clothing at night)

FURTHER READING

The following is a helpful list of useful books, field guides, magazines, and newsletters for the bird photographer. Also listed are Web sites that have become a great resource for photographers. Most photographic magazines have Web sites, as do photographic agencies and individual photographers. There's no substitute for browsing the numerous online publications and resources.

Photography and Nature Photography Books

Debbie Cohen, *Kodak Professional Photoguide*, 6th ed.

Jon Cox, *Digital Nature Photography*

Eastman Kodak Company, *Kodak Guide to 35mm Photography: Techniques for Better Pictures*, 7th ed.

Eastman Kodak Company, *Kodak Pocket Guide to Digital Photography*

Eastman Kodak Company, *Kodak Pocket Photoguide*, 4th ed.

Tim Fitzharris, *National Audubon Guide to Nature Photography*

Lee Frost, *The Question-and-Answer Guide to Photo Techniques*

Tom Grimm and Michele Grimm, *The Basic Book of Photography*, 4th ed.

John Hedgecoe, *John Hedgecoe's Complete Guide to Photography*, revised and updated ed.

John Hedgecoe, *The Photographer's Handbook*, 3rd revised ed.

John Shaw, *John Shaw's Nature Photography Field Guide*

Birding Books

Jonathan Alderfer, ed., *National Geographic Complete Book of Birds*

Jonathan Alderfer, ed., *National Geographic Field Guide to Birds*—state guides currently available for Arizona and New Mexico, California, The Carolinas, Florida, Michigan, New Jersey, Texas, and Washington and Oregon

Mel Baughman, ed., *National Geographic Reference Atlas to the Birds of North America*

National Geographic, *National Geographic Field Guide to the Birds of North America,* 4th ed.

Mel White with Paul Lehman, *National Geographic Guide to Birding Hotspots of North America*

Roger Tory Peterson, *Birds of Eastern and Central North America*, 5th ed.

Roger Tory Peterson, *Western Birds*, 3rd ed.

David Allen Sibley, *The Sibley Guide to Birds*

Birding Photography Books

Tim Fitzharris, *Wild Bird Photography: National Audubon Society Guide*

Tim Gallagher, *Wild Bird Photography*

Arthur Morris, *The Art of Bird Photography: The Complete Guide to Professional Field Techniques*

Arthur Morris, *Bird Photography: Pure and Simple*

Larry West and Julie Ridl, *How to Photograph Birds*

Nature Photography Magazines

Nature Photographer (quarterly)
www.naturephotographermag.com

Nature's Best Photography (quarterly)
www.naturesbestmagazine.com

Outdoor Photographer (10 issues per year)
www.outdoorphotographer.com

Birding Magazines

Birder's World (bimonthly)
www.birdersworld.com

Birding (monthly)
Official publication of the American Birding Association, www.americanbirding.org

Bird Watcher's Digest (bimonthly)
www.birdwatchersdigest.com

Living Bird (quarterly)
Publication of the Cornell Laboratory of Ornithology, www.birds.cornell.edu/publications/livingbird/

WildBird (bimonthly)
www.wildbirdmagazine.com

Birding Newsletters

Backyard Bird News (bimonthly)
Publication of *Bird Watcher's Digest*
www.birdwatchersdigest.com

Winging It (monthly)
Publication of the American Birding Association, www.americanbirding.org

Nature Photography Web Sites

National Geographic Society
www.nationalgeographic.com

National Geographic Photography Newsletter
www.nationalgeographic.com/photography/

Lucid Images Wildlife Photography
www.wildlifephoto.net

National Audubon Society
www.audubon.org

National Wildlife Federation
www.nwf.org

North American Nature Photography Association
www.nanpa.org

Birding Web Sites

ABC Birds
www.abcbirds.org

American Birding Association
www.americanbirding.org

Birds of North America, Cornell University
bna.birds.cornell.edu/BNA

Frontiers of Identification
www.birdingonthe.net/mailinglists/FRID.html

Handbook of Birds of the World
www.hbw.com/index.html

The Virtual Birder
www.virtualbirder.com

ABOUT THE AUTHORS

Rulon Simmons worked for 32 years as an image scientist at Eastman Kodak. He has written and photographed for *Popular Photography & Imaging*, Kodak's *Viewpoints* magazine, *Birds and Blooms*, and *National Geographic BirdWatcher*. His work has also appeared in the books *Winning Pictures*, *Applied Photography*, and *National Geographic Field Guide to Birds* (Michigan, New Jersey, Florida, and California state guides) and has won numerous competitions in the United States and abroad. He lives in Rochester, New York.

Bates Littlehales began profiling birds in 1975 while working on a NATIONAL GEOGRAPHIC article on John James Audubon. Since then he has captured birds in still photography and video. His photographs have appeared in more than 60 publications, including *National Wildlife*, *Natural History*, *Birder's World*, *The Nature Conservancy*, *National Parks*, and *American Heritage*. His books include *Wetlands of North America*, *Bird Watch*, *Wild Southlands*, and the Atlantic Coast and Blue Ridge books in the Smithsonian Guides to Natural America series. He divides his time between the mountains of West Virginia and Virginia's Eastern Shore.

ABOUT THE CONSULTANT

Jonathan Alderfer is the chief consultant for the National Geographic Society's Birding Program. He served as general consultant for the *National Geographic Field Guide to the Birds of North America* (4th edition) and is the former associate editor of *Birding*, the magazine of the American Birding Association.

ILLUSTRATIONS CREDITS

Abbreviations for terms appearing below: (t) top. (b) bottom. (l) left. (r) right. (c) center.
Bates Littlehales/National Geographic Image Collection: 146-147. Bates Littlehales: 2-3, 4, 7, 12, 13, 15, 18-19, 21, 23(t), 23(c), 23(b), 24, 25(t), 25(b), 26, 29, 30, 31, 32-33, 35(b), 36, 44-45, 47, 49, 50, 54-55, 56, 60(b), 64, 67, 68-69, 72, 74, 77, 78, 79, 80, 81, 82(r), 83(t), 83(b), 84-85, 86, 86-87, 90, 96(t), 96(b), 99, 101(t), 101(c), 101(b), 102-103, 104, 106-107, 108, 109, 110(t), 110(b), 111, 112, 115, 118-119, 121, 123(t), 124, 125, 126-127, 129, 130, 132-133, 134(t), 136, 137, 140-141, 142, 143, 144, 145, 149, 152-153, 154, 157, 160, and 166. Bill Hatcher: 42 and 43. Canon USA, Inc.: 38. Heather Hoffman, National Geographic: 9 and 11. Joel Sartore/National Geographic Image Collection: 88. Lynda Richardson/CORBIS: 47. Raymond Gehman/National Geographic Image Collection: 89. Richard Olsenius: 75. Rulon E. Simmons: 14, 16(t), 16(b), 17, 35(t), 59, 60(t), 63(t), 63(c), 63(b), 66, 71(t), 71(b), 82(l), 91, 95, 96(c), 98, 113, 116, 120, 122, 123(b), 134(b), 138-139, 150, 159, 163, and 165. Slim Films: 39 and 40-41. Theo Allofs/Getty Images, cover.

NATIONAL GEOGRAPHIC
PHOTOGRAPHING BIRDS
Rulon E. Simmons with Bates Littlehales

PUBLISHED BY
THE NATIONAL GEOGRAPHIC SOCIETY

John M. Fahey, Jr., *President and Chief Executive Officer*

Gilbert M. Grosvenor, *Chairman of the Board*

Nina D. Hoffman, *Executive Vice President and President, Books & School Publishing*

PREPARED BY THE BOOK DIVISION

Kevin Mulroy, *Senior Vice President and Publisher*

Kris Hanneman, *Illustrations Director*

Marianne R. Koszorus, *Design Director*

Barbara Brownell Grogan, *Executive Editor*

STAFF FOR THIS BOOK

Garrett W. Brown, *Project Editor*

John C. Anderson, *Illustrations Editor*

Carol Norton, *Art Director/Birding Program*

Rebecca Beall Barns, Margo Browning, Susan Tyler Hitchcock, Rebecca Lescaze, *Contributing Editors*

Bob Shell, *Technical Consultant*

Jonathan Alderfer, *Birding Program Consultant*

Jerry Jackson, *Consulting Ornithologist*

Rebecca Hinds, *Managing Editor*

R. Gary Colbert, *Production Director*

Rick Wain, *Production Project Manager*

Teresa Neva Tate, *Illustrations Specialist*

MANUFACTURING AND QUALITY CONTROL

Christopher A. Liedel, *Chief Financial Officer*

Phillip L. Schlosser, *Financial Analyst*

John T. Dunn, *Technical Director*

Vincent P. Ryan, *Manager*

Clifton M. Brown, *Manager*

Founded in 1888, the National Geographic Society is one of the largest nonprofit scientific and educational organizations in the world. It reaches more than 285 million people worldwide each month through its official journal, NATIONAL GEOGRAPHIC, and its four other magazines; the National Geographic Channel; television documentaries; radio programs; films; books; videos and DVDs; maps; and interactive media. National Geographic has funded more than 8,000 scientific research projects and supports an education program combating geographic illiteracy.

For more information,
please call 1-800-NGS LINE (647-5463)
or write to the following address:
National Geographic Society
1145 17th Street, N.W.
Washington, D.C. 20036-4688 U.S.A.

Log on to nationalgeographic.com;
AOL Keyword: NatGeo.

Library of Congress Cataloging-in-Publication Information available upon request.

ISBN 0-7922-5484-8

Photographing Birds is the updated second edition of *National Geographic Photography Field Guide—Birds: Secrets to Making Great Pictures,* originally published in 2002.

Printed in Italy